UNTAMABLE GOD

STEPHEN ALTROGGE

Copyright © 2013 Stephen Altrogge

All rights reserved.

ISBN: 1494448475
ISBN-13: 978-1494448479

DEDICATION

To Jen. I couldn't make it without you.

CONTENTS

1	The God Who Makes Us Feel Warm and Fuzzy	Pg 1
2	The God Who Can't Be Tamed	Pg 15
3	The God Who Speaks Sons and Supernovas	Pg 27
4	The God Who Loves Whores	Pg 42
5	The God Who Kills People	Pg 57
6	The God Who Gives Himself Away	Pg 69
7	The God Who Is Not Impressed	Pg 81
8	The God Who Crushes Serpent Skulls	Pg 91
	About the Author	Pg 102
	End Notes	Pg 103

CHAPTER 1

THE GOD WHO MAKES US FEEL WARM AND FUZZY

I want to warn you up front that these opening paragraphs might sound cynical, jaded, and slightly Scrooge-ish. Please don't throw the book across the room in anger, write me a nasty email IN ALL CAPS, or organize a "Stephen Altrogge Book and Effigy Burn." At least not yet. Give me a few pages to show you where I'm going and to prove to you that I'm not completely cynical and jaded. If, after reading this chapter, you still want to organize a book burn I won't hold it against you. In fact, I'll also provide you with a few 8.5 x 11 glossy photos of me to burn as well. Okay, I just wanted to get that out of the way.

Now, lets begin by stating the facts. Jesus is a white male with long, lustrous hair, nicely tanned, unblemished skin, piercing blue eyes, and a constant wistful gaze. He looks like the kind of guy who might drink a soy latte, shuttle his kids to soccer, dance, and theater in a minivan, and listen to albums that are only slightly mainstream (not that there's anything wrong with any of those things). He is well groomed, an extrovert who is the life of all the parties, and he doesn't cause trouble for anyone. At least, that's how most of the pictures depict Jesus. You know, the pictures hanging on the walls of our churches and decorating the inside of children's Bibles. (Side note: My family has one children's Bible in which all the characters have massive white eyes with no eyelids, which makes all of them look like they've been taking high-grade meth. Weird, right?). He looks like a generally nice guy whom we would trust to watch our children and/or our dogs. He looks pleasant. Kind. Warm. Safe. A white, middle-class, suburban male who keeps his lawn neatly manicured and makes environmentally responsible decisions. "Smile, Jesus loves you," right?

And although most people don't specifically paint pictures of God the Father, we have a fairly good mental picture of what he's like. We tend to think of God as a best friend who's always there for us. He listens sympathetically as we unload our heartaches on him; nodding at the right times; placing a gentle, reassuring hand on our shoulder, handing us a Kleenex when we need to mop up our tears. He always takes care of us, giving us just what we need when we need it. He hugs us when we're sad, lets us scream at him when we're mad, and is just an overall nice God. Yes, nice. That's what God is like. He's not pushy or demanding. He really, really wants us to have a good, safe, warm, comfortable life.

The walls of our houses and churches are plastered with photos of bald eagles with warm, uplifting scripture verses superimposed over the photos. We fill our Facebook feeds with a dizzying array of scriptures, photos, and 10,000 variations of the phrase, "God loves you." When someone is going through a tough time we try to comfort them with well-worn, semi-Hallmarkish phrases. "God won't give you more than you can handle." "God loves you and has a wonderful plan for your life." "Whenever God closes a door he opens a window."

Many preachers today make millions of dollars telling

people God loves them and has a wonderful plan for their lives. Every week Joel Osteen tells thousands of people that their best days are right around the corner. That every day should be like a Friday. That God always, always, always has a new, bright, beautiful, shining, healthy, zestful, financially lucrative future in store for them. That every Christian should be constantly living the victorious, triumphant, kick-butt and take names life. That if you don't have perfect health, a great sex life, success on the job, and honor roll children then you're missing out on what God has for you. That, just as the Beatles said, "You've got to admit it's getting better, getting better all the time." Millions of Christians tune in to this message every week, eating up the sermons and podcasts and Tweets and blog posts of these passionate prosperity preachers. They come away feeling better about themselves, better about life, and better about God. The "every day a Friday" gospel is well and alive in America and throughout much of the world.

The Christian music scene isn't helping things much either. Many Christian songs, including worship songs, could easily be directed to a girlfriend or boyfriend with a few simple tweaks (most people don't say "Hallelujah" to their significant others). Churches gather together every Sunday and sing chipper, happy, upbeat, uplifting, always positive, family-friendly songs, complete with ambient lights and, possibly, fog machines. Worship leaders in tight jeans and v-neck t-shirts bounce up and down, clutch the microphone in dramatic Bono fashion, and tell everyone to join hands and dance in the river.

I warned you that I might sound jaded and cynical. But I'm not. Really. I too believe in a God who does good things for his children. I too believe in a God who loves to bless. I too believe in a God who meets us in the midst of our darkest night. And I'm not trying to mock or smear those of you who post happy photos on Facebook. I'm not trying to mock Christian music. In fact, I'm a worship leader who happens to like a lot of happy, upbeat songs. I encourage people to sing enthusiastically and joyfully. I can't stand it when bands try to out-angst each other. This book most certainly will not be an outraged manifesto in which I rage against the church, capitalism, cheesy music, and hypocrisy. I love the Church and I love my local church. More importantly, I believe Jesus loves the Church and cares very much about the state of the Church. Jesus calls the Church his bride, and only a fool would rip on Jesus' bride. If you want to make a guy angry start insulting his wife. If you want to make Jesus angry start insulting his bride.

This book is not a call for people to leave their local churches. This is not some sort of epic rant calling for sweeping reform in the church. This is not one of those "Un" books in which I tell everyone to become an "Unchristian" in an "Unchurch" for the glory of "UnJesus." I don't see myself as a modern day prophet predicting the impending doom of the Church. Let me say it loud and clear: I LOVE MY CHURCH AND JESUS LOVES THE CHURCH.

My main concern is that we as Christians (and I include myself) have put God into a box. We have tamed God. Domesticated God. Shackled God. Caged him. Made him fit into a mold of our own making. We don't see God as he truly is. We have smeared our already dim mirrors with a veneer of our own ideas. We have made God safe, comfortable, easy, and accessible, as if he exists to serve us and make us happy. He is like a comfort blanket to us. He is a divine butler who promptly responds to our every beck and call, a glorified genie who likes to grant us wishes. Each of our boxes looks a little different, but all of us have stuffed God into a box.

If we're honest with ourselves, most of the time we would rather keep God tame and in his box. When God is tame and in his box, we can understand him, control him, and keep him at a safe distance. When God is tame, we can neatly compartmentalize him, categorize him, dissect him, and analyze him. When God is in his box, we can keep him out of certain areas of our lives. We can keep him in his place. We can do what we want. There is no mystery when God is tame and in his box. There is no overwhelming awe or gut-check fear when God is in his box. God in a box. It sound likes a toy you might purchase for your nephew or niece. "Come on down to Toy-O-Rama and get a pet God-in-the-box!"

It's time to let God out of his box. It's time to meet the God who cannot be tamed.

Why are so many young people leaving the Church? I'm sure there are studies and statistics that spell out the reasons in bar graphs and bullet points, but I don't think the answer is that complicated. The reason so many people are leaving the Church is that God seems irrelevant to them. They see God as existing to meet their needs and make them happy. And sure, God can make them feel good, but so can a lot of other things. Making piles of money feels good. Climbing the corporate ladder feels good. Buying a motorcycle and spending your days cruising around the country feels good. Ski trips feel good. iPhones, iPads, XBoxes, and Playstations feel good. I'm not saying these things are inherently wrong, but if God is simply one option on a buffet, why stick with God?

Why do our devotional lives so often seem tepid, frustrating, and even boring? Again, I don't think the answer is complicated. We have reduced God to a set of formulas, trite phrases, and well-worn Bible verses. We have reduced God to "Footprints in the Sand" and the serenity prayer and "Got Jesus?" t-shirts. We have made God such a bore! There is no thrill in serving a "Footprints in the Sand" God. God carried me when things got tough. Whoop-de-doo. I once talked to a girl who said the band Radiohead carried her through a lot of tough times. Serving a "Got Jesus?" God doesn't require steely nerves and great courage. Why should we bother with such a boring, cheesy, shallow, lame God? There's a reason people jump off cliffs, skydive, and visit the Grand Canyon. We want to be captivated. Thrilled. Blown away. In awe. Swallowed up by the greatness of something or Someone else. Personally, I'm not all that interested in serving a boring God.

A.W. Tozer spoke directly to this problem when he said:

> The Church has surrendered her once lofty concept of God and has substituted for it one so low, so ignoble, as to be utterly unworthy of thinking, worshipping men...With our loss of the sense of majesty has come the further loss of religious awe and consciousness of the divine Presence. We have lost our spirit of worship and our ability to withdraw inwardly to meet God in adoring silence.[i]

In other words, we have tamed God and put God into a box. And there is no room for majesty, awe, or a sense of the divine Presence in this box.

Now, just to make it clear that I'm not a heretic, I don't believe God can really be tamed or put into a box or reduced to boring nothingness. God is who he is regardless of what we think about him. He is reality. All other realities are derived from him. God is the great I Am, and nothing I think, say, or do can reduce his earth-shattering glory. You can no more contain God than you can contain the sun.

But, if we want our churches to thrive and our devotional lives to flourish, we absolutely *must* let God be God. We cannot settle for warm, fuzzy, "feel good movie of the year" versions of God. We cannot settle for a God who exists only to meet our needs and make us happy. We cannot settle for a God who is boring and irrelevant. We cannot settle for a God of our own imagination. We must know the ferocious, untamable God. We must let God out of the boxes we have created. We must come face to face with God as he really is, with all his sharp edges and blazing glory and heart-rending beauty. We must encounter the God who makes mountains melt like wax and the angels cover their eyes and the rivers leap for joy. If we are going to love God with all of our heart, soul, mind, and strength, we must truly know God. We must know him as he truly is, not as we imagine him to be. We must come to grips with the God who has revealed himself in scripture.

As Francis Chan said in his book *Erasing Hell*, too often we apologize for God. When we come to hard parts in the Bible we stumble and bumble and try to explain God away. We try to explain away a God who sends people to Hell. We try to explain away a God who kills people. We try to explain away a God who is described in the Bible as consuming fire and unapproachable light. We try to explain away a God who makes angels tremble and demons shudder. The God revealed in the Bible doesn't fit neatly into our boxes and categories. The God of the Bible can't be neatly summarized in bumper stickers or t-shirt slogans. The God of the Bible can't be psychoanalyzed and quickly diagnosed. We don't want a God who makes us feel uncomfortable. We want a God who is all warmth, smiles, happiness, and hugs. When God doesn't fit that description we apologize for him. We make "yes, but" statements. "Yes, God is wrathful, but he really is a God of love."

It's time to stop apologizing for God.

The great revivals of the past have come when God's people recovered a true, lofty, grand, thrilling, entrancing, fascinating, frightening, biblical vision of God. Jonathan Edwards' sermon "Sinners in the Hands of An Angry God" portrayed a God who was not love, love, love, and nothing but love. Regarding those who continue to reject God, he said:

> They are now the objects of that very same anger and wrath of God, that is expressed in the torments of hell. And the reason why they do not go down to hell at each moment, is not because God, in whose power they are, is not then very angry with them; as he is with many miserable creatures now tormented in hell, and there feel and bear the fierceness of his wrath. Yea, God is a great deal more angry with great numbers that are now on earth; yea, doubtless with many that are now in this congregation, who it may be are at ease, than he is with

many of those who are now in the flames of hell. So that it is not because God is unmindful of their wickedness, and does not resent it, that he does not let loose his hand and cut them off. God is not altogether such a one as themselves, though they imagine him to be so.

Wow. I'm not sure if I would have the guts to unleash such a shotgun blast of fury and wrath upon my congregation. In our politically correct culture, these words seem intolerant, narrow-minded, and unloving. A God who is angry? Surely not! I don't believe in a God like that. I believe in a God who accepts everybody just as they are. I have one of those religious symbol "Coexist" bumper stickers on the back of my Subaru. At first glance these words can seem harsh, angry, and vindictive, but Jonathan Edwards wasn't angry or vindictive toward the members of his congregation. He wasn't a revival tent preacher who stumped back and forth across the stage and railed against the evils of dancing, playing cards, and theater-going. Rather, he wanted his congregation to come face to face with the holy, righteous, consuming God of the Bible so that they might repent of their sins and turn to God for salvation. He wanted the members of his congregation to experience the deep, perplexing, overwhelming love of God. However, he knew they would never experience the love of God if they didn't first feel the immense, intense, burning wrath of God. Jonathan Edwards did not apologize for the wrathful side of God, just as he never apologized for the loving side of God about which he so often wrote and spoke.

The results of this sermon were astonishing. God unleashed the Holy Spirit. Hundreds of people fell under deep conviction of sin and turned to God for forgiveness and salvation. Revival burned through the community, and men and women who were formerly apathetic toward God were seized by a great zeal for God. Entire communities were transformed and revitalized. Jonathan Edwards let the untamable God out of the box and the people in his church were never the same.

If we're going to make a difference in the world for Jesus we too must encounter the wild, untamable, consuming, holy, righteous, loving, compassionate, merciful, wrathful, just, pure, good God of the Bible. We serve a God who is not like us. A God with sharp edges and strong opinions. A hurricane of a God. A tsunami of a God. A God who is greater, more loving, more just, more furious, more frightening, more delightful, and more tender than we could possibly imagine. A God who can't be contained in neatly packaged phrases. A God who breaks our vocabulary. A glorious God. A thrilling God. An infinitely exciting God. We can't afford to lose sight of that God. We can't settle for low, lousy, cheap ideas of God. We can't settle for secondhand, shrink wrapped, processed ideas of God.

In Philippians 3:8 the Apostle Paul said, "Indeed, I count everything as loss because of the surpassing worth of knowing Christ Jesus my Lord." Paul was willing to throw aside everything he had in order that he might know Jesus Christ. He was willing to sacrifice his reputation, health, comforts, friends, and ministry success, if only he could know Jesus Christ. Before becoming a Christian, Paul was a mover and a shaker in the Jewish religious society. He was the young phenom Pharisee. The religious Rookie of the Year. He had the adoration of his peers and was on the fast track to being a religious celebrity of sorts. Jewish mothers told their sons to be like Paul when they grew up. So what changed? Jesus caught Paul with a left hook of blinding light, knocking him off his horse. As he lay on the ground, Paul caught a glimpse of the real Jesus, and that glimpse ruined him for anything else. Only a colossal view of God and Christ and the Holy Spirit could inspire such whole-hearted, pedal-to-the-metal devotion in Paul. Paul had encountered the living Christ, and he knew that Jesus surpassed everything else. Jesus made everything else look like trash. Like loss. Like dung. Paul had been captured and captivated by a true vision of Jesus.

We have two options. We can settle for a boring,

uninspiring, tepid relationship with God, in which we come to church, sing a few songs, and go about the rest of our lives. Or we can pursue God in all his grandeur, glory, and captivating beauty. To choose the first option is a travesty. God is GOD! To settle for anything less than a true, glorious, exalted vision of God is utterly stupid and utterly sinful. God wants to invade our lives, turn them upside down, shake us to our core, undo us, rebuild us, love us, change us, and unleash us on the world. Why would we dare settle for anything less? God doesn't want to inhabit a little cubby hole in our lives. He doesn't want two hours on Sunday and one hour on Wednesday night. He wants all of us.

We too must encounter the real Jesus, just as Paul did. If God is going to make any real difference in our lives, and if our churches are going to have any lasting impact on the world, we must be willing to let go of our safe, comfortable, tame, fuzzy ideas of God and come face to face with the God of the Bible.

In his wonderful book *Knowing God*, J.I. Packer wrote:

> What makes life worth while is having a big enough objective, something which catches our imagination and lays hold of our allegiance; and this the Christian has, in a way no other man has. For what higher, more exalted, and more compelling goal can there be to know God?[iii]

My generation is desperately trying to make sense out of life. They are groping and grasping for meaning, caught in an endless existential cycle that leaves many of them despairing and cynical. They don't have an objective bigger than their own happiness and satisfaction and self-fulfillment. They don't have anything bigger than themselves to catch their imaginations. They stumble from one thing to the next without having any grand sense of purpose or direction. We are a generation of wanderers and waifs, of strugglers and stragglers, blown from one thing to the next, always searching but never finding. Just like Bono, we still haven't found what we're looking for.

In an interview with "The Guardian," pop megastar Lady Gaga described one of her recent tours as a "religious experience" for her fans. What sort of religious experience is she giving to her fans? "It's more self-worship, I think, not of me. I'm teaching people to worship themselves."[iii]

Lady Gaga, along with thousands of other pop icons, is selling self-worship. In his most recent album, *Yeezus*, Kanye West blatantly states that he is a god. He clarifies that he is not as high as God himself, but a god nonetheless. This is the message that is being enthusiastically embraced by my generation. We are all gods. We are all worthy of worship. We are all worthy of glory, praise, and admiration. We are the center of our own personal universe. We create reality. You are a god. I am a god. We are all gods! We are the captains of our souls. We are our own supreme reality. We must follow our hearts, choose our own adventure, and find our calling.

It's all a terrible, unsatisfying, life-destroying lie. God never intended us to be at the center of anything. In fact, God created us in such a way that we can never satisfy ourselves. No matter how much inner exploration, self-worship, or self-fulfillment we experience, we simply cannot satisfy ourselves. Whether we climb to the top of Maslov's hierarchy of needs or the top of the business world, the results are the same. When we put ourselves at the center, everything falls to pieces. Only God has enough gravitational pull to keep us in the proper orbit. When we become the center, everything begins to spiral out of control. In *The Courage to Be Protestant*, David Wells wrote:

> The self that has been made to bear the weight of being the center of all reality, the source of all our meaning, mystery, and mortality, finds that it has become empty and fragile. When God dies to us, we die in ourselves.[iv]

We who are Christians have the answer to the question, the cure for the infection, the true North direction. We know the true and living God, the Exalted One, the most compelling, interesting, wonderful, glorious person in the universe. However, we aren't going to effectively reach my generation until we are freshly wrecked by a vision of our God. My generation can smell hypocrisy and artificiality a mile away. They have a sixth sense which allows them to sense when a person's words are hollow. Shallowness is the ultimate turnoff for my generation. When we truly meet God and are gripped by God's glory and captured by his majesty and overwhelmed by his holiness and decimated by his justice and caught up in his tenderness, our words about God will not be hollow. They will be overflowing with life and love and passion and affection.

Every couple of years someone writes an alarmist, slightly apocalyptic book or blog post predicting the death of the Church. "The Church is losing its influence on the world!" they cry. "All of our current ways of doing church are failing. We need to scrap everything we are currently doing and return to the model of the early church!" Honestly, I don't buy it. The Church has been gaining influence and losing influence since it began 2,000 years ago. The early church had its strengths and weaknesses. There were lots of signs and wonders performed in the early church. There were also lots of heretics invading the early church. Yes, we should always be concerned for the Church and desiring to see it prosper. But the success of the Church depends on Jesus, and Jesus has not abandoned the Church. He will ensure the continued growth of the Kingdom of God. And the reality is, the early church had just as many weaknesses as the modern church. The Corinthian church was like a frat party compared to some of our modern church services.

The early church did have one significant strength, however: It was keenly aware that God was real and that God was active. For the first Christians, Jesus was not simply one small facet of their incredibly busy lives. He was not a slot in their calendars. He was their life. In Acts 2:42-47 we read this description of the early church:

And they devoted themselves to the apostles' teaching and the fellowship, to the breaking of bread and the prayers. And awe came upon every soul, and many wonders and signs were being done through the apostles. And all who believed were together and had all things in common. And they were selling their possessions and belongings and distributing the proceeds to all, as any had need. And day by day, attending the temple together and breaking bread in their homes, they received their food with glad and generous hearts, praising God and having favor with all the people. And the Lord added to their number day by day those who were being saved.

This is a picture of a church that is alive, vibrant, zealous, disruptive, and edgy (in the good way, not the "Hey look, I'm awesome," way). This is a picture of Christians who have encountered the untamable God. Awe and wonder was upon every soul. They didn't cling to their possessions or hoard their food. They encountered the real, living, miracle-working, life-changing Christ on a daily basis, and those regular encounters energized and animated them. The early Christians were a definite threat to the religious status quo.

I don't think the church is dying. I don't believe we should abandon our churches and start monastic communes in the wilderness. I love the Church universal and I love my church in particular. My church is full of godly people who are living lives that truly please God. But sometimes I wonder if we have lost the wonder and awe and intensity which characterized the early church. There are certainly times when I put God into a neat, easily understandable, safe box. When I put God into a box my relationship with him suffers. I lose the holy recklessness that characterizes those who encounter the living God.

I could close this chapter by making a cliché statement about beginning a journey into wonder, or some other mystical nonsense that sounds poetic, but doesn't mean whole lot. But the point of this book is actually pretty simple. I'm writing it for myself. I want to meet God in all his majesty and be freshly undone by his glory. I'm also writing it to you, so that you may also encounter our incredible, glorious, untamable God.

CHAPTER 2

THE GOD WHO CAN'T BE TAMED

I was a business major in college so allow me to put my degree to use for just a moment. Mom, dad, if you're reading this please take note. All that money you spent on me wasn't a total waste.

In the business world there exists a certain type of person called a "venture capitalist." Venture capitalists are the people who supply money to startup companies. When a young college dropout comes up with the next Facebook or Google, venture capitalists will be the ones who help the company get off the ground. The truth is, most entrepreneurs are young, poor, driven, semi-educated kids who have brilliant ideas and zero cash. Hence the need for venture capitalists.

But the harsh reality is that venture capitalists are ruthless. They have to be. Every year, they receive thousands of pitches from hungry entrepreneurs, desperate to get the funding they need. The capitalists have to be able to distinguish between the next Google and the next Google Buzz (a Google product that was a total bomb). They have to be able to quickly separate the Facebooks from the "you've got to be kidding me's." And so each venture capitalist has a checklist of things a company must have before he will even think about writing a check.

Now here is where my business background and theological background intersect. I'm pretty sure I could be a religious venture capitalist. In other words, if you wanted to start a brand new religion I would be the guy who supplied the funding. Because when it comes down to it, I know what makes for a successful religion. Yes you need the rituals and the special holidays and holy sacraments. You need the sacred garments and religious jargon. You need the pilgrimages and the relics and the spiritual heroes. However, none of these things are what is most important. For a religion to really thrive it must offer its most devoted followers the opportunity to become a god of some sort.

Think about it for a moment. Mormonism tells its devotees they will someday rule planets. Joseph Smith, the founder of Mormonism, said, "God himself was once as we are now, and is an exalted man, and sits enthroned in yonder heavens." In other words, God was once a human like us, and someday we too might become a god like him. If you pay your Mormon dues and wear your sacred Mormon undergarments and do a two-year mission trip you've got a decent chance at godhood. Shoot for the stars. Literally.

Scientology makes similar promises. If a person performs enough "auditing" sessions (you'd think they could come up with a catchier name - that's something I'd address as a venture capitalist) they can attain a state of exaltation, enlightenment, and god-like status. Why do so many celebrities get sucked into Scientology? Because it gives them a chance to rise even higher than they already are. They are already gods in our culture. Scientology offers them the chance to be gods of the cosmos.

Most religions offer the promise of exaltation or secret

knowledge or nirvana or absorption into the divine consciousness. If you play your cards right and perform your rituals correctly, you can shed your worthless earthly body and become a god. If I'm going to give you money to create a startup religion you better offer me a shot at becoming a god.

Which, of course, is why I would never offer money to a person trying to pitch me on Christianity. Christianity is different from so many world religions. Yes, it does promise that the longer we know God the more we will become like him both in character and action. However, the Bible makes it crystal clear that I am not God, I will never be God, and God is infinitely greater than me. There is an infinite gap between God and me. No matter how much I do, no matter how many rituals I perform, no matter how much secret knowledge I gain, I will never be God. God is not a man and a man will never be a god.

As Christians, most of us know this, yet so often we think of God as simply being a much more powerful version of us. We have some knowledge; God has a lot more knowledge. We have some strength; God has much more strength. We are loving; God is much more loving. We are big; God is a lot bigger. You get the point.

The problem with this line of thinking is it puts God in a cage. It tames him. Limits him by the fences of our imaginations. Yes, it's true that as God's image bearers we share some of his attributes, but scripture makes it clear that God is not like us. He's not a bigger, better version of us. God is not a 2.0, new-and-improved deluxe version of us. He is *infinitely* greater than us. Wholly Other than us. He is a God who decimates our imaginations and obliterates our tiny conceptions of him.

Isaiah 55:8-9 says:

> For my thoughts are not your thoughts, neither are your ways my ways declares the Lord. For as the heavens are higher than the earth, so are my ways higher than your ways and my thoughts than your thoughts.

In these verses God takes a chainsaw to any lofty ideas we have about ourselves. It's as if he's saying: "Oh you think you're kind of a big deal? You think you're a big shot? You think you know how I work? You don't know jack. Let me tell you a thing or two about me."

God starts by dismantling our intellect. He says, "My thoughts are not your thoughts." In other words, God does not think like us. His way of thinking is completely different from ours. Our minds operate one way; God's mind operates on a completely different level. It's not like we're at a community college and God is at an Ivy League school. It's like we're at a community college and God comprehends all the mysteries and mechanics of the entire universe. We don't even operate in the same stratosphere as God.

There are some pretty smart people in the world. Geniuses. Prodigies. People who comprehend things like quantum physics and genetic manipulation and atom splitting. People like Stephen Hawking, Albert Einstein, and Marie Curie. These are the kind of people who break standardized tests. The world adores people like this. We worship the IQ. We stand in awe of astronomically intelligent people. When I compare myself to men like Stephen Hawking, I am deeply aware that I am an idiot. I have a difficult time understanding the inner workings of a combustion engine, let alone quarks, parsecs, and the time-space continuum.

When I was a freshman in college I took an intro to earth and space class. On one of the first days of class, an older woman ("non-traditional student" is the politically correct term) stood up and asked if we would be studying something called "string theory" which was advocated by a man named Brian Greene. I could tell she was bedazzled by Brian Greene and wanted us to be bedazzled by the fact that she had read Brian Greene. I wasn't bedazzled. Frankly, I don't give a rip about string theory or alternate universes or parallel dimensions. That stuff is way over my head and it makes me feel confused and stupid whenever someone starts talking about it. My fellow non-traditional student, however, was very enamored with the genius of Brian Greene.

But God is not impressed with the geniuses of the world. He informs us that his thoughts are not our thoughts. In fact, our deepest thoughts, most intelligent ideas, and most profound ponderings are tiny, insignificant, and rather childish when compared to the infinite intelligence and wisdom of God. God's overwhelming, all-encompassing knowledge makes the computations of Stephen Hawking look like crude crayon drawings. God's baffling brilliance makes Einstein's greatest ideas seem childish, immature, and stunted. As high as the heavens are above the earth, so God's thoughts are higher than ours. This is a metaphor. It doesn't mean God's thoughts are exactly 26,345.7 miles higher than our thoughts. It means God's thoughts tower infinitely above ours, just as the heavens seemingly stretch into infinity.

Consider and be flummoxed by the great expanse of our God's knowledge. Scripture says he calls each and every star by name. This implies God has an intimate knowledge of every single star in the entire universe. I can keep somewhere between five and seven things in my memory at one time. If I try to remember any more than that, my synapses begin to short circuit and burn out. God knows each of the trillions of stars which fill the universe by name. He holds them all in his consciousness simultaneously, managing them, speeding up the atoms of some, slowing down the cosmic energy of others, directing each one on its appointed celestial path. He knows which ones will blossom into supernovas and which ones will simply fade away. He directs the paths of the planets, meteorites, and black holes, like a beautiful cosmic symphony. The sun and moon and galaxies and supernovas and meteor showers all declare the infinite wisdom of God. God lifts his hands and solar flares joyfully leap forth from the sun. He snaps his fingers and stars fade to black. He flicks his fingers and meteorites trace their way through the earth's atmosphere. The universe is God's orchestra. If all the knowledge in the universe were a circle, the sum total of human knowledge would be a faint speck in that circle.

Every year, scientists release studies informing us that certain things are good for us. Drinking a glass of wine every day is heart healthy. Drinking eight glasses of water per day promotes healthy skin. A diet high in fiber promotes colon health. And though I'm grateful for the men and women who devote their lives to studying the human body, these studies can be incredibly frustrating. Why? Because every few years a new study is released which contradicts everything in the older studies. Everything we thought we knew turns out to be incorrect. For being the most intelligent species on the planet, we humans are actually pretty stupid. Compared to the living God, our intelligence is incredibly low and limited.

And it's not just that God knows a greater quantity of information than us, like a teacher knows more than a student. His way of thinking about things is vastly different than ours. His thoughts are wholly other than our thoughts. We process things one way, he processes things a completely different way.

When I make a decision, I try to consider various factors. How will this decision affect my budget? Do I have time to do this? How will this affect my children? The more factors go into a decision the more stressful that decision becomes. I think this is why buying a car is so stressful. I wander into a car dealership, and in less than fifteen seconds a salesman has me in an all-out interrogation. Do I want front wheel or rear wheel drive? Do I want good gas mileage or a large engine? Do I want the optional three-year protection plan which is valid only on Thursdays and only in states starting with the letter "W"? My brain is so limited. The more options thrown at me, the more panicky I become.

When God makes a decision, he considers all of history past, all that is currently occurring in the world, and every event which will occur in the future. When God ordains a thunderstorm in Iowa he is also aware of the traffic patterns in Melbourne, the inflation rate in Argentina, and the prayers of a six year-old in China. God knows all things at all times, and his decisions take every possible factor into account. He. Doesn't. Make. Mistakes. So often my decisions are like shots in the dark or a dart thrown while blindfolded. I hope I make the right choice, but my decision making ability is so tiny, so infantile, and so blind.

The colossal dot-com bust of the early 2000's is proof of just how pathetic and piddly we really are. Thousands of young men and women started tech-based companies, and for a short time it appeared that they were geniuses. They created intricate, detailed business plans, harnessing all their knowledge and creativity in an effort to create the perfect company. For a brief time they were on top of the world, making millions of dollars and establishing themselves as the Jedis of Silicon Valley. Then everything went to hell in a virtual shopping cart. People realized MySpace wasn't so awesome after all and that they didn't need 8,300 free hours of America Online. All the best laid plans of the whiz kids turned out to be connect-the-dot pictures in which all the wrong dots were connected. Millions were made, millions were lost, millions were humbled.

Compare this to what God says about himself in Isaiah 46:9-10:

> ...for I am God, and there is no other; I am God, and there is none like me, declaring the end from the beginning and from ancient times things not yet done, saying, 'My counsel shall stand, and I will accomplish all my purpose,'...

Are you starting to get the picture? God is not like us. His ways are not our ways and his thoughts are not our thoughts. He cannot be neatly summarized or contained. He cannot be reduced to formulas or theories. All the scientists and philosophers and theologians and pastors and punks cannot begin to fathom or understand the immensity of God. Our highest, deepest, loftiest thoughts of God only scratch the surface of his overwhelming glory. If you think you've got

God figured out, you're worshiping the wrong God. He makes geniuses look like fools and the most brilliant philosophers sound like blathering buffoons. He knows all that has been and all that will be, and absolutely nothing can stop him from accomplishing his breath-taking purposes.

Some of you are the planning type. You got a DayTimer for your 12th birthday. You have your days planned to the minute. You have your weeks planned to the day. You have your years planned to the week. And you have your life planned to the year. Checklists are your lifeblood and to-do lists give you a contact high. Overall your life feels stable, planned, and under control.

Except when it's not. When all your best laid plans get washed away like a sandcastle in the tide. When you lose your job. When you get throat cancer. When your kid ends up in prison. When your husband cheats on you. When your 401(k) gets decimated. When everything you've built and worked toward comes toppling down in a heartbreaking heap.

No matter how meticulous our planning, there will be many times when life feels like a sucker punch to the head. When life doesn't make sense. When life feels like a hurricane. When we want to curl up into the fetal position and die. It's in those times we need a God who can't be tamed or caged or kept in a box. We need a God who is not like us. We need a God who doesn't think or act or work like us. We don't need a warm cuddly God who gives us a shoulder to cry on. We don't need a God who leads us in the serenity prayer. We need a colossal, sovereign, ruling, reigning, good, tender, and merciful God. We need a God who doesn't operate according to our standards. We need a God who knows what he is doing! We need a God who was willing to kill his Son on our behalf.

The cross is the greatest proof that God does not think or act like us. The cross is evidence that God's ways are infinitely higher and better than ours. The cross is a sledgehammer to all our preconceived notions about God. The cross strips away the curtain and reveals God in all his blinding majesty.

The cross shows us what God is really like.

At the cross we see an impossible problem and a startling solution. The problem is this: how can wicked, rebellious, sinful men and women like you and me be reconciled to a holy, pure, righteous God? God's holiness is no joking matter. When the angels cry, "Holy, holy, holy, is the Lord God Almighty," there is no irony in their song. They're not singing a barroom ditty. They are proclaiming reality. Sin is the antithesis of God. It is the opposite of all that is good and just. God abhors sin. We are full of sin. God's holiness and our sinfulness create an impossible dilemma.

The greatest minds in history have tried to solve this divine dilemma, and almost all of them have arrived at the same solution: man earning his way to God. All the rituals, all the good deeds, all the striving for nirvana boil down to man working his way to God. That's the best we could come up with. But this solution doesn't even begin to address the problem. This solution makes a mockery of God's holiness and justice. God is a consuming fire and a righteous judge. He can't simply let bygones be bygones. He can't sweep our sins under the rug. Wickedness demands justice. God's holiness demands perfection. If we have to earn our way to God, then we are jacked seven ways to sideways.

When a man rapes a child, we are appalled. When a dictator slaughters innocent people, we are outraged. When a shooter walks into a school and mows down children and teachers, we are furious. When a terrorist detonates a bomb at the Boston Marathon, we scream for justice. When we see a bully taking advantage of a young child, we feel anger surging through us. Our sense of outrage, fury, and anger are a faint taste of how God feels toward sin. God hates sin. It makes him sick and angry and furious. God can't simply dismiss our sin any more than we can dismiss the crimes of a rapist or terrorist. How can God forgive our sins and still execute justice? All our attempts to solve this divine dilemma have been spectacular failures. We've managed to come up with pilgrimages, relics, cleansing rivers, prayers to the east, and fire dances. But relics and rivers and dances cannot cleanse the conscience. A deeper magic is needed.

Only God himself could devise a way for divine justice and divine mercy to walk hand in hand. Only a God whose ways are not our ways could devise a plan that could both satisfy his holy justice and allow him to forgive those who have so grievously offended him. The cross is a visible demonstration of God's deep, unfathomable wisdom.

2 Corinthians 5:21 says, "For our sake [God] made [Christ] to be sin who knew no sin, so that in him we might become the righteousness of God." The Son of God became a man, lived a life of perfect righteousness, then died in our place. Jesus satisfied God's holy wrath for our sins and he freely gives his perfect righteousness to us.

No human could devise such an audacious, brilliant, creative plan. Only a God who is not like me could come up with such a solution. This is why Paul says:

> For Jews demand signs and Greeks seek wisdom, but we preach Christ crucified, a stumbling block to Jews and folly to Gentiles, but to those who are called, both Jews and Greeks, Christ the power of God and the wisdom of God. For the foolishness of God is wiser than men, and the weakness of God is stronger than men. (1 Corinthians 1:22-25)

To the Jews the idea of a crucified Messiah was blasphemous. They wanted a conquering, crusading, warrior Messiah who would crush their Roman oppressors and establish himself as a holy king in this world. A crucified man was a man condemned by God. The idea of a crucified Messiah? Impossible. Unthinkable. Utterly ridiculous. God would never do such a thing.

To the Greeks the idea of a crucified Messiah was laughable. The Greeks respected men who were powerful leaders and masterful orators. The idea of God himself becoming a man, making himself a servant, then dying on a cross was absolutely ludicrous. Where was the power? Where were the brilliant campaign speeches? Where were the pomp and circumstance and victory parades? A dying God? A servant God? That's a grand joke indeed.

...Unless it so happens that God's ways are not our ways and his thoughts are not our thoughts. That kind of God would die on a cross for me. That kind of God would take my sins upon himself. That kind of God would make himself nothing, becoming a servant, in order to rescue me.

I can trust a God who would kill his Son for me. As Romans 8:32 says, "He who did not spare his own Son but gave him up for us all, how will he not also with him graciously give us all things?" God did the unthinkable and impossible for me. If he went to such great lengths to save me will he hold any good thing back from me?

My knowledge is so limited and finite, and there are times when life is so confusing and overwhelming. There are times when life feels like a hurricane and a knockout punch and a shot of Novocain. There are times when everything seems to go dark. When there is no light at the end of the tunnel. When it feels like I'm experiencing some sort of divine blackout. But in the midst of all the confusion and chaos I have one, unshakeable anchor: God gave up his Son for me. If God could solve the greatest problem, then surely my problems are not too much for him to handle. If God could cross the uncrossable divide between Him and me, then he can certainly manage any problems I encounter. I don't know the end from the beginning, but I know the One who has already written the end and the beginning, and I know he is trustworthy.

If I were running the show I probably wouldn't choose to bring certain circumstances in my life. But if I were running the show, I wouldn't have chosen the cross either. Needless to say, it's a good thing I'm not running the show.

God cannot be tamed. He simply does not fit into my box. His thoughts are infinitely higher than mine, his ways infinitely better. And so I rest in this God. Trust him even when life doesn't add up. Humble myself before him. And shut my mouth.

CHAPTER 3

THE GOD WHO SPEAKS SONS AND SUPERNOVAS

We artists have a somewhat well deserved reputation as being sensitive souls. We protect and defend our work with a ferocity more commonly associated with soldiers under heavy fire and/or a mother bear protecting her cubs. If someone criticizes our painting or poem or essay we vehemently insist that they just don't get it. We go to great pains to explain that the painting of an apple isn't just a painting of an apple. It's so much deeper and more profound! The apple, which, admittedly, looks exactly like an ordinary apple, really represents the ongoing battle between capitalism and socialism. And that mountain in the background isn't just any old mountain. It's symbolic of the rise of the modern man. The critic is obviously blind to the beautiful essence of our art. He is an uncultured swine who should spend his time watching NASCAR instead of pretending to be an art critic. Let the reader understand: when you criticize someone's art, you should expect the artist to get huffy.

When parody specialist Weird Al Yankovic wrote a parody of Coolio's hit rap song "Gangsta's Paradise," Coolio was furious. He felt Yankovic had desecrated his song by transforming the epic "Gangsta's Paradise" into the hilarious "Amish Paradise."

While I feel the word "desecrated" might be a bit strong (we're talking about a song, not the Mona Lisa), I can relate to Coolio in a few small ways. First, I wish I had a rap name like "Coolio" or "Bu$ta Pound." That, however, will have to wait for my autobiography, which will be written under a rap artist pen name. In case you're wondering, the title of my autobiography will be *Quiet Mediocrity: The Incredible True Story of a Middle-Class Kid Who Didn't Achieve Too Much*. It will be a shocking tell-all you won't want to miss.

I can also relate to Coolio's ferocious possessiveness of his creative work. These words and sentences you're reading are mine. They originated in my brain. They were transferred from my brain to my computer by my fingers. They mean a very specific thing. I don't want anyone rearranging or deleting any of these words. I don't want any hand-drawn illustrations added. This book is my creation and it exists for a very specific purpose. If you're one of those post-modern readers who thinks he can interpret my sentences however he wants, then you need to put this book down and go to a poetry slam or something. This book is mine and I decide why it exists. I am the creator and this is my creation. Got it? Good.

Why all the ranting and raving and foaming at the mouth? Why the sudden explosion of artistic mother bear instinct? Why all the huffing and puffing and throwing wild punches? The reason I'm so worked up is, we live in a culture which passionately insists we are autonomous beings. We are the captains of our souls, the directors of our destinies. Woe to the man who limits our self-expression. Woe to the woman who hinders our self-actualization. Teachers and mentors and even pastors are hell-bent on helping us find ourselves. Writers and life-coaches and existential gurus encourage us to create our existence and to shape our identities. To live our dreams. To fulfill our deepest potential. To make a grand bucket list. Ten-thousand times a day we are told that we are at the center of our own personal universe, and everything must revolve around us. We're all on a grand journey to the center of ourselves, searching for hidden treasure deep within the mines of our souls.

All this personal backslapping and self-huzzah-ing and "we're so awesome"-ing would be fine and dandy, but for the fact that it ignores one monumental truth: we are creations.

If, by some miracle of time prestidigitation, I created myself, then I would be free to chart my own destiny. As I said earlier, the creator determines the purpose of his creation. But I did not create myself. God did. Yes, my parents came together and did their part in bringing me into existence. But as anyone who has battled the demon of infertility knows, there is no guarantee that a sperm will successfully impress an egg. And even if the sperm and egg actually do pair up (provided the egg's father gives the sperm permission) there is no guarantee that the uterus will play along. For all these things to happen in the proper order, a divine miracle must occur. The gears of our DNA must align perfectly. Our X and Y chromosomes must divide into even teams. The head bone must be connected to the neck bone must be connected to the arm bone. The tiniest malfunction in any of these processes could result in us being born with a deformity or not born at all. We are created. God is creator.

King David was keenly aware of this fact when he wrote:

> For you formed my inward parts; you knitted me together in my mother's womb. I praise you for I am fearfully and wonderfully made. Wonderful are your works; my soul knows it very well. (Psalm 139:13-14)

It was God who brought the sperm and egg, which were the beginning of me, together. It was God who wound strands of DNA together, which would result in me having brown hair, gray eyes, and a skinny-ish (as I get older my body is becoming more "ish" and less "skinny") body. It was God who fused neurons and synapses and gray matter together into a brain which would allow me to snap my fingers and make a jump shot and line a single to left field and play a C chord on my guitar. It was God who paired my chromosomes together. It was God who strung tendons between my knees and knuckles. It was God who connected my eye to my optic nerve to my brain.

"Fearfully and wonderfully made," is an enormous understatement. God could have ended my life shortly after I was conceived. He could have allowed my umbilical cord to wrap around my neck. He could have allowed me to be born with a fatal genetic defect. I suspect heaven will be filled with children whom God called home before they ever made it out of the womb, but that's for another book.

My point is this: we are all works of art. Not in a "we are all special snowflakes, we are the world," sort of way, but in a "God made us and you better believe we belong to him" sort of way. We are God's creations. Because God made us, he owns us. We are God's possessions. I am not the captain of my soul or the decider of my destiny. God is. The artist always owns and decides the fate of the artwork.

My generation is constantly being told how important we are. We are told to pursue our dreams, to follow our hearts, to choose our own adventures. Everybody is making bucket lists these days - checklists of things they want to do and experience before they die. We make these extensive, audacious lists as if we have a divine right to experience everything we want before we die. I want to bungee jump. I want to go to Africa. I want to run a marathon. I want to learn to fly. I want to see the pyramids. Don't tell me what I can and can't do. If I want to go fly fishing on the Amazon River, by golly I'm going to fly fish on the Amazon River.

My generation is being sold on a lie.

If we're going to truly know and understand and love God we must come to terms with the fact that he is Creator and we are creations. He is infinitely above us. We are servants and he is the King. We belong to him in every sense of the word, and he has absolute prerogative over us. The Potter shapes the clay into whatever sort of vessel pleases him. He picks up a lump of clay and slams it down onto the sculpting wheel. He pushes it and punches it and softens it. As the clay spins in front of him he carefully presses and bends and molds the clay. The Potter has a vision in his mind's eye and is determined to make that vision a reality. A cup cannot suddenly decide it wants to become a bowl. A plate cannot protest, "Why have you made me this way?" The Potter is in command, shaping and molding and massaging the clay. The clay submits to the skillful touch of the Potter. The story submits to the grand imagination of the Author. The canvas submits to glorious vision of the Painter. We are the clay, the story, and paint.

In Genesis 1:27 we read, "So God created man in his own image, in the image of God he created him; male and female he created them." We are created in the image of God. The image of God has been branded upon us, leaving a holy scar. To be made in the image of God is no small thing. The glorious, burning, brilliant angels are not made in the image of God. None of the animals are made in the image of God. We humans have the incredible honor of being made in the image of God, and with this incredible honor comes incredible responsibility.

God made us in his image in order that we might represent him on the earth. God has commissioned us to be his vice-regents, representing his rule and reign on the earth. We are to rule over creation as God rules over creation, stewarding and working the earth in a way that honors God, blesses others, and respects the wonderful world God has created. We are to be a small yet visible demonstration of what God is really like. This is why God said to Adam and Eve, "Be fruitful and multiply and fill the earth and subdue it, and have dominion over the fish of the sea and over the birds of the heavens and over every living thing that moves on the earth." (Genesis 1:28) We are to be fruitful and multiply in order that the glory and image of God can spread throughout all the earth. The more people fill the earth, the more the image of God fills the earth. We are to subdue the earth and have dominion over it in order that the image and rule and reign of God can spread through all the earth.

This job description is not optional. God is the creator, and he created us for a very specific, intentional purpose. He created us in order that his image might go viral, filling every nook and cranny of the earth with his glory. God didn't create Adam and Eve, dust off his hands, and then say, "Welp, my work is done, go make something of yourselves." God didn't command Adam and Eve to find self-fulfillment and happiness, as wonderful as those things are. He didn't command them to find their best life now. He didn't command them to follow their hearts. He commanded them to spread his glory and fame and image throughout all the earth. Period.

God is creator. He formed Adam from the dirt, animated the dirt, then gave Adam a divine commission. And that same commission applies to us. We too are called to represent the living God wherever we are, to spray and spread his glory wherever we go. This isn't one of many choices. This isn't like one of those career aptitude tests in which you find out you're best fitted to be either a teacher, a plumber, or a world leader. This isn't like one of those old *Choose Your Own Adventure* books where, depending on the choices you made, the book could have a happy ending or a sad ending. God has already chosen our adventure.

When Moses encountered the living God at the burning bush God said to him, "Do not come near; take your sandals off your feet, for the place on which you are standing is holy ground." (Exodus 3:5) Moses' bare feet touching the earth was a reminder that he was a creature standing in the presence of his Creator. Moses, like Adam, was a man formed from dust, who would eventually return to dust. Before God sent Moses on his truly epic mission of leading the Israelites out of Egypt, God wanted to remind Moses of creaturely status. Moses was God's creation, and as such, had to obey God no matter what the cost.

We would be wise to take our shoes off more often. To remember our lowliness. To remember the frailty of our frame. To ponder the vast gap that separates us from our Creator. To stand in awe of the One who spoke planets and kangaroos and phytoplankton into existence. To humble ourselves in the presence of the One who keeps our hearts pumping and our synapses firing.

In Psalm 90:12 Moses wrote, "So teach us to number our days that we may get a heart of wisdom." I don't like visiting nursing homes. In fact, I feel distinctly uncomfortable in nursing homes. I look around and see people who have pretty much reached the end of their days. Men and women who were once full of energy and life and ambition, are confined to recliners and wheelchairs. Great thinkers and doers who have been betrayed by their bodies. When I see elderly men and women, I'm reminded of just how brief and brittle life really is. And yet there is wisdom in numbering our days. Numbering our days reminds us that we're creatures who have been allotted a short time upon this earth. I don't want to waste the little time I have. I want to spend my life fulfilling the mission God has given me. We need to regularly take our shoes off and feel the earth between our toes. To wander through cemeteries and ponder all those who have gone before us.

I'm currently sitting in a coffee shop. My brain is struggling to put flesh on the bones of my ideas. There are times when inspiration blows up in my brain like a firecracker, but for the most part creating things is hard. Writing requires a concerted effort on my part, and I'm constantly hitting the "delete" button because my words sound like something composed by a hyperactive four year old. And I'm not alone in my creative struggle. Thomas Edison spent thousands and thousands of hours working on the light bulb. The light bulb! A small piece of glass containing a simple piece of burning filament. Hemingway rewrote the ending to *A Farewell To Arms* 39 times. The reason? He had trouble coming up with the right words.[v]

God doesn't struggle with creator's block. I write a sentence, scratch it out in disgust, and say, "This is crap." God speaks a word, the galaxies blossom, and he says, "This is good." A painter dabs color onto a canvas, steps back, surveys her work, then takes a knife to the canvas in disgust. God dabs the barren earth, causing flowers, fig trees, and rain forests to burst forth. He steps back, surveys his work, and says, "This is good." A sculptor pushes and pounds his clay, desperately trying to wrestle it into submission. He places the molded clay into a kiln, solidifying his efforts. He removes the hardened, glazed clay, looks at it closely, then hurls it across the room in frustration. God takes raw earth between his fingers, breathes upon it, and says, "It is very good." God's first drafts are always flawless. He thinks, speaks, and it is good. He creates reality, and it is always very, very good.

Stop for a moment and flex your fingers. Notice how your fingers bend and clasp at the bidding of your brain. Bend your knees. Feel the rough concrete beneath your bare feet. Listen to your heart do its bass drum routine, laying down the backbeat of your life. Inhale deeply. Notice the panoply of smells that assault you. See your chest expand and feel your ribs creak as your lungs fill with oxygen. How is this biological circus possible? A million different incredibly intricate things are happening simultaneously in your body right now. Blood is being rushed throughout your body. Stop that flow for more than a few minutes and you will die. Increase that flow just a bit and you'll have a brain aneurysm, also causing you to die. Your eyes receive a thousand different impulses every second, which are then carried along your optic nerve to your brain, which somehow manages to make sense out of the jumbled mess. Every second of your life is a performance of epic proportions. And this performance is not just happening in you. The same extravagant circus is repeating itself again and again in billions of people around the world. A production of this magnitude must have a Ringmaster of infinite capability. You and I would be crushed by the sole task of maintaining our heartbeat. God maintains billions of heartbeats without a second thought. He is the Grand Ringmaster and we are his sacred circus. He is the Creator and we are the creation.

Stories are a hot commodity these days. Everybody and their evil step-mother has written a memoir. Seemingly everyone has a sprawling story of survival, triumph, and loss. Every event, no matter how mundane or trivial, must be reported in breathless, self-congratulatory tones. And, of course, contained within these numbingly mundane events are profound life lessons which must be impressed upon others. In my humble, non-literary expert opinion, autobiographies tend to focus more on the facts of a person's life, with the occasional profundity sprinkled in for good measure. Memoirs, on the other hand, are all about stories and "aha!" moments and self-discovery. Some authors have written three, four, or even five memoirs. And we bloggers are no better. We're always writing posts with titles like, "6 Profound Life Lessons I Learned While Waiting In Line At The DMV."

While I'm all for telling stories, our fundamental temptation is to become obsessed with *our* story, as if ours were the one that mattered most. But consider for a moment all the stories that have come before us. Billions of men and women have already lived out their stories. Stacks and stacks of people have worked difficult jobs, become kings, made love, made war, made a fortune, birthed children, lost children, grown old, and eventually returned to the ground. The reality is, our stories only take up a few, brief sentences in the massive book of history. Maybe we're not all special snowflakes after all.

So do our stories even matter? Yes, but not in the way we think. Our stories matter because they are a part of God's grand story. We are all characters in God's sprawling four-part saga entitled *HISTORY*. This saga, which unfolds as

"Creation", "Fall", "Redemption", and "Consummation", truly is the greatest story ever written. It includes angels, demons, prophets, a dragon, a curse, a tragedy, a rescue, and above all else, a Hero. The story has been millennia in the making. If you don't know the ending I won't spoil it for you other than to say the good guy wins.

The fact that we are part of God's story once again brings us face to face with the reality that we are creatures. God has given each of us a role to play in his glorious story. Each of us has been given lines and scenes and entrances and exits. Some of us will play multiple roles. Some of us will step into tragic scenes and some of us will step into comedic bits. Some of us will play starring roles and some of us will be in the supporting cast. Some of us will have more lines and more of the spotlight than others, but given the significance of the story, we all better play our parts to the hilt.

I realize that by speaking like this, I risk sounding fatalistic, which is anathema in our, "Give me liberty or give me death," culture. But the wonderful reality is our stories are not really our stories, they are God's. This reality loads our lives with meaning and frees us from the exhausting task of trying to feel important. Because we are God's creatures, every thing we do is important! When Shakespeare said, "The world is a stage," he was dead on. God has placed each of us on this spinning terrestrial ball and given each of us a part to play in the glorious story he is writing.

Our opening lines are found in 1 Corinthians 10:31, which says, "So whether you eat or drink, or whatever you do, do all to the glory of God." We are born, God hands us those lines, then cries, "And...action!"

Every moment of our lives is fraught with divine importance. Eating oatmeal matters. Drinking your second or third or fourth cup of coffee matters. Going to the dentist and changing diapers and creating spreadsheets and doing homework all matter. We exist to bring glory to God in everything we do. Every morning is a new scene in God's glorious story. God is keenly interested in everything we do.

He is the Creator and we are his creations. He is the Director and we are the actors. The actors don't get to make up their lines or scenes. They can't see the big picture. They don't know how the story ends. When an actor goes rogue and starts making up lines, he ruins the beautiful story. When each actor starts doing his own thing, it trashes the entire story. God is the glorious director and we sure as Hell (literally) better not try to take his place.

Of course, there is such a thing as an awful story. You know the kind of book or movie I'm talking about. The dialog is stilted, the characters one-dimensional, and the ending unsatisfying. These are the kind of books we want to chuck across the room when we finish reading the last sentence. The authors of these stories obviously have no idea what they're doing.

But the Author of our stories knows what he's doing. He's not a two-bit hack writer pumping out pulp novels. He's not bumbling his way through a plot, trying to figure out what comes next. He already has the plot figured out. He knows how our story and all the other stories are going to come together in the end. He's a master craftsman, an artisan of cosmic proportions. He's the Sovereign One, the King of Kings, the Lord of History, the Alpha and Omega.

There will be many times when our story doesn't make sense. When the plot takes an unexpected twist, leaving us gaping and gasping for breath. When everything unexpectedly fades to black, we will say to God, "Why did you do this? Do you have any idea what you're doing?"

And he will say to us:

> Who is this that darkens counsel by words without knowledge? Dress for action like a man; I will question you, and you make it known to me. "Where were you when I laid the foundation of the earth? Tell me, if you have understanding. Who determined its measurements— surely you know! Or who stretched the line upon it? On what were its bases sunk, or who laid its cornerstone,

when the morning stars sang together and all the sons of God shouted for joy? (Job 38:1-7)

Too often we forget who we're really dealing with. We do all the right things. We read our daily devotionals and go to church and listen to positive, upbeat, family-friendly Christian radio. And these things are all fine and good, but they're also very safe. It's easy to trust God when things are safe. It's easy to be creatures when everything is going our way. I think God lets things spin out of our control to remind us of who is really in charge. To remind us of who is really God. To remind us of just how helpless and dependent upon him we really are. We question God and he speaks to us out of the whirlwind, saying, "Where were you when I was creating the world and all the angels were harmonizing my glories? Are you really going to question me, your Creator? Do you really have the audacity to raise your fist to me? Do you think you could do a better job of running the world? Do you want to try your hand at writing the story?"

And then God will speak to us again, this time in a softer voice which cracks with emotion. "Where were you when I hung my Son upon the judgment tree? Where were you when I unleashed all my abhorrence and hatred toward sin on my Son? Where were you when I turned my back on him, leaving him hanging in the blackness of my judgment? Where were you when he screamed out in desperation and despair? Where were you when the spear punctured his side and the remnants of his life trickled out?"

If God were all power and no love, he would be a terrifying God. Being a creature would be a hellish, horrifying existence. We would have no guarantee that God would not smite us, reducing us to ashes and dust. We would have no hope of forgiveness or redemption.

If God were all love and no power, he would be a useless God, wanting to help us but unable to do so. He would be nothing more than a divine comfort blanket.

But the God we serve is a magnificent, breathtaking,

mind-befuddling combination of love and power. He is not part power and part love. He is not sorta loving and sorta powerful. He is omnipotent and omniloving.

We can trust and love and stand in silence before our omnipotent, omniloving God. How great is his power? The galaxies, planets, and dark matter all follow the course traced by his finger. The sun sprints across the sky, joyfully running the race marked out by its Maker. Swallows and crickets and falcons and angels sing themselves hoarse in joyful adoration of God. The atoms in my body jostle about at just the right speed, fast enough to keep me from freezing to death and slow enough to keep me from bursting into flame.

> O Lord my God, When I in awesome wonder,
> Consider all the worlds Thy Hands have made;
> I see the stars, I hear the rolling thunder,
> Thy power throughout the universe displayed.

How great is his love? His love is so great he became like us. The Son of God, eternal in existence, omnipotent in power, worshiped by angels, feared by demons, entered into our story. Divinity was wrapped in fragile flesh. Without losing any of his divinity he allowed himself to be limited. His omniscience was limited by the ball of flesh housed in his skull. His omnipotence was fenced in by a body that fell asleep in the back of boats. The Sovereign One, the Maker of All Things, the Star Sustainer became a baby boy with grasping fingers and a soft spot atop his head.

And then, mystery of mysteries, the God-man Jesus allowed himself to be arrested, mocked, covered in mucus, beaten to a pulp, hung on a cross, and finally crushed by the wrath of God for sins he did not commit.

Why would the Son of God allow himself to be humiliated in such an awful manner? Why would the commander of angel armies allow himself to be destroyed in such a horrible fashion? Why would the One adored by angels allow himself to be mocked, spat upon, and sucker punched?

He allowed it in order that we, lowly, rebellious creatures, might become sons and daughters of the living God.

And when I think, that God, His Son not sparing;
Sent Him to die, I scarce can take it in;
That on the Cross, my burden gladly bearing,
He bled and died to take away my sin.

What sort of God do we serve? Certainly not one who can be tamed or boxed or fully understood. Don't get me wrong: I'm all for precise theology and sound doctrine. Squishy, undefined theology is a breeding ground for heresy. But if we're not careful, the regular handling of sacred truths can slowly diminish our capacity for awe and make us think we've got our minds around God.

We need to be regularly reminded we are creatures. Remembering our creatureliness should have two wonderful effects on us. First, it should humble us. We're not as awesome as we thought. We do not chart our own destiny. We do not exist independently. We are created beings who are sustained every moment by our Creator. Every talent and ability we possess is a gift from God to be used for God. Can you breathe? That is a gift. Can you walk? That is a gift. Can you play the piano? Gift. Hit a baseball? Gift. Preach? Gift. Weld? Gift. Organize data? Gift. If God were to stop sustaining you for a second, you would dissolve into nothingness. Our existence, and every wonderful thing which comes with it, are all gifts from our Creator. As Paul says in 1 Corinthians 4:7, "What do you have that you did not receive? If then you received it, why do you boast as if you did not receive it?"

Acknowledging that we are creatures and God is our Creator allows us to humbly, gratefully receive and enjoy the gifts he has given us. It also reminds us of our rightful place in the universe. Every day we are tempted to believe the universe revolves around us. We are tempted to act as if everyone and everything should do our bidding. But we are not God. God is God, and everything revolves around him. We cannot demand from God. We cannot rant and rail and rave against him when things don't go our way. God is God and he is free to do as he pleases. Remembering that we are creatures should push us to our knees in humble adoration of our Creator.

Second, remembering our creatureliness should make us feel very, very loved. This is not, "You're good enough, you're smart enough, and people like you," talk. This is not a rallying call to more self-esteem. We are created in the image of God. We are stamped with the divine. This fact alone makes us valuable. My value does not come from my job, my looks, my sense of humor, or my social status. My value comes from the sacred truth that I am created in the image of the living God.

And to top it off, I am also bought with the sacred blood of Christ. God owns me twice: once by creation and once by redemption. God's double ownership of me is a deathblow to insecurity and the fear of man. I don't need the approval of others to be secure because I have the approval of God. God loves me because I am created in his image and because I am wearing the righteousness of his Son. I can rest in that. I can stop trying to be somebody because I already am somebody.

God is not like me, and that's a very good thing. He doesn't fit into my little box. He is the Creator and I'm the creature. Knowing that I'm a creature allows me to stop striving for worldly greatness and to worship the One who is truly great.

CHAPTER 4

THE GOD WHO LOVES WHORES

Once upon a time there was a kingdom. In this kingdom lived a young woman named Cinderella. Her life was simply dreadful. Her father died when she was young, and she was forced to live with her wicked step-mother and awful step-sisters. They treated her like trash, forcing her to do menial housework and never letting her have any fun. Her step-mother and step-sisters locked her in her room every night while they went out and partied. Her step-mother and step-sisters ate organic food and forced her to eat food from Wal-Mart. Her step-mother and step-sisters used Apple products and forced Cinderella to use Microsoft products. Every night, Cinderella cried herself to sleep. She desperately wished someone would rescue her out of her horrible life.

In this kingdom there also lived a prince named Prince (his father was a big fan of the other "Prince"). Prince was a noble, virtuous, brave, hard-working young man. There was just one problem: he couldn't find a girl to marry. He had read all the right dating books and had even created a profile on ChristianMingle.com, but he still couldn't find the right girl. All the married women in his church shook their heads when they saw him because he was such a nice young man and he deserved a beautiful girl. One day, in an effort to help his son, Prince's father decided to host a ball at his castle. All the girls in the entire kingdom were invited to the ball. *Surely my son will find a wife now*, thought Prince's father.

Through a series of very fortunate events involving a fairy godmother, a pumpkin, a healthy dose of magic, and a glass slipper, Prince and Cinderella met. They danced, they kissed, they fell in love. After a very short courtship (Prince always did things by the book), Prince and Cinderella were married. Everyone was happy for Prince because he found the girl of his dreams and everyone was happy for Cinderella because she was rescued out of her terrible situation. And Prince and Cinderella lived happily ever after.

Until Cinderella cheated on Prince and slept with another man.

Prince was heartbroken that the girl of his dreams had cheated on him. Cinderella was rightly ashamed of her despicable actions and begged Prince to take her back. Prince still deeply loved Cinderella and agreed to take her back. They kissed each other tenderly, and from that moment forward they lived happily ever after.

Until Cinderella cheated on Prince again. This time she hooked up with someone through Facebook.

Once again she pleaded with Prince to take her back, and once again he did, welcoming her with love and tenderness.

But something was fundamentally wrong with Cinderella. She could not stop cheating. She was addicted to affairs. She cheated on Prince again and again in worse and worse ways. With each betrayal, Prince was more heartbroken. What had become of the girl of his dreams?

Finally, Prince had no choice but to force Cinderella out of the castle. Cinderella lived on the streets, selling her body to the highest bidder. Prince spent his days locked in his castle, and eventually he died of a broken heart. And nobody was happy ever again.

Pretty awful story, right? There's a reason Disney always stops at the happily ever after part. That's what all of us want - to live happily ever after. But the story of the adulterous, cheating Cinderella is actually a true story. It's the story of Israel in the Old Testament. It's also my story and your story.

The story begins at the very beginning with Adam and Eve. God created the first couple and placed them in the Garden of Eden. He loved them dearly and they loved him. He walked with them, talked with them, and had sweet, uninterrupted fellowship with them. But the fellowship was broken when the shifty, power hungry serpent entered the garden. Like every shady salesman, the serpent promised Eve something better than she had. And like every shady salesman, the serpent failed to live up to his promises. Nonetheless, Eve believed the serpent's lie and ate from the forbidden tree. She cheated on God. Adam should have made his stand against the serpent and fought to the death, but he didn't. He also cheated on God. God was heartbroken.

But God was determined to have a people for himself, a bride, if you will. So he called a man named Abram to himself, and God made Abram some incredible promises. Abram would have many children, Abram would have a place to call home, and Abram would be a blessing to all the nations. A son was born to Abram, and sons were born to that son, and sons were born to the sons. God's people, who were called Israelites, were growing, and everything seemed to be going well.

Then, in a macabre plot twist, the Israelites became slaves of the Egyptians. They were forced to do backbreaking labor. They had no land of their own. They weren't a blessing to the nations. Rather, they were cursed by the nation of Egypt. When the Israelite population kept growing Pharaoh ordered all male Israelite babies be killed. The Israelites sighed and groaned and called out to God for deliverance.

God heard the cries of the Israelites and his heart was tender toward them. He raised up a man named Moses who would lead the Israelites out of Egypt. Then he wreaked havoc upon the Egyptians, hitting them with bloody water, hail, locusts, flies, gnats, darkness, and even death itself. Finally, when Egypt was in shambles and Pharaoh couldn't take it any more he let the people of Israel go.

As God led the Israelites through the desert, he continued to do incredible things for them. He annihilated the Egyptian army in the Red Sea. He created weather patterns of bread and created water-giving rocks. He kept their sandals from wearing out.

God tenderly cared for the Israelites as a groom cares for his bride, and in return, he asked Israel to obey the commands he gave them. In Exodus 19:5-6 God said to the people of Israel:

> Now therefore, if you will indeed obey my voice and keep my covenant, you shall be my treasured possession among all peoples, for all the earth is mine; and you shall be to me a kingdom of priests and a holy nation.

Israel would have a special place in God's heart. They would be his precious, treasured possession. They would have a unique relationship with God. They would be a kingdom of priests, a holy nation. Out of all the nations of the earth, Israel would be God's chosen, treasured people. God bestowed incredible privilege upon Israel.

God didn't ask Israel to sacrifice their children in return for such incredible blessings. He didn't command them to offer human sacrifices on mountain peaks or to throw virgins into volcanoes. He simply asked for their love and obedience. And Israel swore up and down on their mothers' graves that they would love and obey God. Exodus 19:8 describes the people's response to God's request: "All the people answered together and said, 'All that the LORD has spoken we will do.'"

Everything seemed to be going very, very well. God had his people and Israel had their God. Israel would be a light to the world, showing the world what the true God was like. But there was something fundamentally wrong with the people of Israel. Despite all their promises and oaths they could not obey God. God's first command to the people of Israel was that they must not worship any other gods. Israel was surrounded by nations who worshiped false gods. The true God, the God who had dramatically rescued Israel from Egypt, the God who had proven himself to be the true and only God again and again, would not have his people worshiping false gods. In Exodus 20:3-4 God said to Israel, "You shall have no other gods before me. You shall not make for yourself a carved image, or any likeness of anything that is in heaven above, or that is in the earth beneath, or that is in the water under the earth. You shall not bow down to them or serve them, for I the LORD your God am a jealous God..."

The reason God didn't want the Israelites making or worshiping carved images was, he could not be sufficiently represented by a carved image. The glory and majesty and power and love and ferocity and humility and tenderness of God could not be captured by any sort of image created by a person. Any attempt to represent God by an image would actually be a colossal insult to God. It would be like if I asked you to paint a portrait of my beautiful wife and the picture turned out to be very ugly. It would be an insult to me and my wife.

This seems like a reasonable request, doesn't it? God was simply asking the people of Israel to reserve their worship and honor for the true God. He was asking them to worship him only. He was asking them not to insult his glory by making carved images of him. This request was one he had every right to make. He had done everything for Israel. He had rescued them, healed them, provided for them, led them by pillars of fire and smoke, triumphed over Egypt and all its false gods, and proven again and again that there was no god like the true God. The people of Israel had seen God descend on Mount Sinai. They had felt the mountain shake and rattle and roll. They heard the terrifying divine trumpet blast announcing God's arrival at Sinai. For Israel to give their love and worship to any other false god would be adultery of cosmic proportions. For Israel to worship any other God would be abominable and revolting.

Yet Israel quickly abandoned God. When Moses went up on Mount Sinai, the people said to Aaron, "Up, make us gods who shall go before us. As for this Moses, the man who brought us up out of the land of Egypt, we do not know what has become of him." (Exodus 32:1) When Aaron heard this request, he should have said, "What are you talking about? Are you smoking crack? Have you already forgotten what the true God has done for us? Do you think I can manufacture a god? There is only one God and I won't profane his name by trying to create a god for you." But Aaron didn't utter a word in protest. Aaron had seen God in action. He had seen the Nile go blood red and heard the buzz of millions of locusts. He knew God was real and should have defended God against the people of Israel. Instead he created a golden calf for the people to worship. The people of Israel gave their hearts in worship to a lifeless hunk of gold formed into the shape of a cow. Instead of loving the God of fire and smoke and trumpet blasts and plagues and water from rocks and bread from heaven, they loved a lifeless piece of gold. They prostrated themselves before a cow.

God was heartbroken and furious and wrathful and sorrowful. His bride had cheated upon him. His treasured people had abandoned him and profaned his name. He had every right to destroy them. He had every right to obliterate them, along with the rest of humanity, from the face of the earth. He had every right to call flaming chunks of brimstone down upon them. But he didn't. He punished Israel but he did not abandon Israel. The greatness of his love and forgiveness and tenderness kept him from abandoning his treasured people.

You would think the people of Israel would have learned their lesson after their first affair. But they didn't. They abandoned God again and again, worshiping false gods, marrying foreign women, and even offering up their children in sacrifice to demons. God would punish the people for their adultery, allowing them to become slaves of foreign nations. Then the people of Israel would cry out to God in repentance, and God's merciful heart would melt once again. He used judges and prophets and kings and donkeys to rescue them from their oppressors.

But Israel was addicted to worshiping false gods. They couldn't stop injecting false religion into their veins. No matter how many times God rescued them, they always returned to their false gods, like dogs returning to vomit. Finally, God allowed the people to be taken captive by the nation of Babylon.

In Ezekiel 16:15-22, God said to the people of Israel:

> But you trusted in your beauty and played the whore because of your renown and lavished your whorings on any passerby; your beauty became his. You took some of your garments and made for yourself colorful shrines, and on them played the whore. The like has never been, nor ever shall be. You also took your beautiful jewels of my gold and of my silver, which I had given you, and made for yourself images of men, and with them played the whore. And you took your embroidered garments to cover them, and set my oil and my incense before them. Also my bread that I gave you—I fed you with fine flour and oil and honey—you set before them for a pleasing aroma; and so it was, declares the Lord GOD. And you took your sons and your daughters, whom you had borne to me, and these you sacrificed to them to be devoured. Were your whorings so small a matter that you slaughtered my children and delivered them up as an offering by fire to them? And in all your abominations and your whorings you did not remember the days of your youth, when you were naked and bare, wallowing in your blood.

You can hear God's heartbreak and sadness and fury and sorrow and exasperation in these verses. His beloved bride, Israel, had become a spiritual whore. Like prostitutes pulling tricks, the Israelites threw themselves at every false god that came their way. Israel took the gold and silver God had given them and turned them into false gods. Israel took the precious children God had given them and offered them up as burning sacrifices to demons. In spite of God's overwhelming affection for and favor toward Israel they constantly abandoned the God of their youth. In spite of the fact that God rescued Israel from their enemies again and again they continued to run after foreign gods.

It's easy to judge the people of Israel. To act all high and mighty and holier-than-thou. To climb up on our soapboxes and proclaim our superiority. Surely we would never do what they did. Surely we would never be so foolish as to worship an idol made out of gold. Surely we would never offer our children as sacrifices to false gods. We're better than that. More civilized. More cultured. More righteous. Right? Wrong. The same evil that lurked in the hearts of the people of Israel lurks in our hearts as well.

These days it's cool for Christians to talk about how everyone is broken. The world is a messed up, broken place. All of us are hurt and broken people. Jesus is the Great Healer who meets us in our brokenness. And there is some truth to all the brokenness banter that gets tossed around. But I've got a problem with using the word 'broken' to describe what is wrong with the world and with me. Brokenness doesn't even scratch the surface of what is truly wrong with us. Is a rapist simply a broken person? Is a child pornographer just broken? Is a CEO who abandons his family for his career only broken? Is a pastor who laps up praise like a thirsty dog simply broken? Is a man who destroys his family so he can have sex with his secretary just broken? The reality is, apart from God, we aren't just broken, we're evil. Our souls are bent and twisted and gnarled. We are not shining beacons of goodness. We don't gravitate toward goodness and charity and love and kindness. We don't naturally move toward God and his ways. We gravitate toward slander and anger and addiction and lying and porn and self-gratification.

Jeremiah 17:9 describes our natural state of being apart from God: "The heart is deceitful above all things, and desperately sick; who can understand it?" Not broken. Not wounded. We're talking deceitful above all things, desperately sick, and incomprehensible. Why would a man ruin his marriage by looking at porn? Because our hearts are deceitful above all things. Why would a woman constantly criticize and nag her husband? Because our hearts are desperately sick. Why would a young man call his mother a bitch and his father an idiot even though they have showered love and affection upon him? Because our hearts are sinfully irrational. We are way more than broken. We are way more than wounded. Apart from God's supernatural work, we are all wicked and evil to the core.

The reason people like Billy Graham attract so much attention is because people like him are so rare. Self-sacrificing, loving, serving people are a rare commodity. We instinctively know we should be like Billy Graham and we instinctively know we are not like him. We are self-worshipers through and through. We may not worship golden images but that doesn't mean we're not idol worshipers. We worship idols of comfort, money, sex, popularity, security, rest, children, social status, sports, and a million other things.

In Romans 3:10-18 we read the following description of humanity apart from God:

> "None is righteous, no, not one; no one understands; no one seeks for God. All have turned aside; together they have become worthless; no one does good, not even one." "Their throat is an open grave; they use their tongues to deceive." "The venom of asps is under their lips." "Their mouth is full of curses and bitterness." "Their feet are swift to shed blood; in their paths are ruin and misery, and

the way of peace they have not known." "There is no fear of God before their eyes."

This description isn't hyperbole. God isn't using extreme, shock-jock language here. This is God's fair, calculated assessment of the human race. And if you think this is an unfair description, then you haven't taken an honest look at yourself. You know the secret thoughts and desires that course through you. You know the hatred and arrogance that fills your heart. You know the perverse sexual desires that arrest you. You know the words you have said about others. You know how easily you become consumed with your career or your appearance or your bank account or your popularity. You know how difficult it is to put someone else's interests ahead of your own. Don't get me wrong, you're no worse than anyone else, but you're also no better. Don't try to hide behind a veneer of niceness. God isn't impressed by niceness. God sees right through the niceness to the depths of your heart.

Let's come right out and state the truth: apart from God, I am evil and you are evil. Our hearts are bent toward wickedness. We are flat-out rebels against God.

Why all this talk about evil and depravity? Why so much macabre introspection? You didn't start reading this book so you could be reminded of how awful you are. And generally speaking, making broad sweeping statements about our wickedness doesn't sell a whole lot of books. So what's my deal? Am I one of those people who takes some sort of sick pleasure in feeling bad about myself? Am I a masochist who enjoys inflicting pain on myself?

The reality is, we will never understand the profound depths of God's love for us until we first understand the profound depths of our own wickedness. If, like me, you grew up in a church, this can be tough to grasp. I don't have a crazy testimony. I wasn't addicted to meth at the age of twelve. I was never in a gang. I didn't grow up in the projects. I never got involved in really serious, awful sin. I was the kid who won all the Bible quizzes in Sunday school. I was a nice, generally polite, middle-class kid. But prior to God saving me, my heart was full of wickedness.

We will never grasp the height and depth and breadth of God's love for us until we first come to terms with who we really are apart from God. The men and women who have loved God the most are those who have been the most aware of their own sinfulness and the depths of God's forgiveness.

If a man came to you and told you his wife cheated on him, what would you tell him? If she cheats once, you might tell him to hang in there. You might encourage him to forgive his wife. To try and make amends. If she cheats a second time, you tell him to at least consider separating for a time. But if she cheats a third time? You tell him to get out of that toxic marriage. You tell him to divorce his wife and have nothing to do with her. Only a naive fool would stay with a wife who is a serial cheater. The repeated pain and heartbreak and betrayal would be too much for anyone to bear.

So why hasn't God washed his hands of us?

Luke 7 tells the story of a Pharisee named Simon. Simon threw a dinner party and invited Jesus to attend the party. Now, you need to understand something about Simon. He was a very moral, religious, upstanding guy. He was a Pharisee, which meant he was devoted to the Mosaic Law. His entire life and worldview were built upon his own morality and righteousness. His very identity was wrapped up in being religious. And Simon wasn't the kind of guy who hung out with people from the bad side of the tracks. Simon spent his time with other moral, upstanding people.

Simon's dinner party was interrupted by an unexpected guest: a woman with a really sleazy reputation. Luke 7:37 says she was a "sinner." This doesn't mean she was a sinner in the sense that we are all sinners, it means she was a really sinful sinner. Moms told their children not to be like this woman when they grew up. She was the kind of woman who went to great lengths to seduce men. She was a marriage wrecker. She reveled in sexual immorality. A trail of ruined lives lay behind her. She was a whore, literally and spiritually.

And yet. God, the Hound of Heaven, began to hunt her. He began to press upon her wounded heart, squeezing until the bittersweet bile of conviction bubbled to the top. He created loving, divine chaos in her life, turning her assumptions upside down and ripping her sinful cocoon to shreds. He stripped away all her excuses and exposed her soul to his holy, convicting light. By the time Simon's party rolled around the woman was a mess. Her conscience was raw. She was deeply aware of her wickedness and deeply aware of her need for forgiveness.

And so she came to Jesus. She barged into Simon's party without asking permission and went straight for Jesus. She fell at his feet, weeping under the weight of her sins, and then began to wipe his dirty feet with her hair. She poured expensive perfume upon him. She had no doubts about her spiritual condition. She wasn't trying to maintain a veneer of goodness. She was keenly aware of her wickedness, and she knew she needed forgiveness and mercy. This ritual was her way of asking forgiveness. She was demonstrating her repentance for all to see and smell.

Simon didn't like what he was seeing. He cringed at all the weeping and wiping and perfume pouring. It made him feel very uncomfortable. He was a Pharisee. He did all the religious stuff. He worshiped in the synagogue, tithed down to the penny, memorized the Torah, and did his best to obey every one of the 613 commands given by God to the people of Israel. He would never have let a prostitute near him, let alone wipe his feet with her hair. He was a "holy" man, and holy men didn't associate with prostitutes or drunkards or tax collectors.

But Simon had a problem. He didn't truly understand God. He couldn't understand a God of scandalous love and grace. His God-box didn't have room for grace that welcomed prostitutes. His God-box didn't have space for forgiveness that could cleanse even the worst of sinners. And so Jesus said to Simon, "Therefore I tell you, her sins, which are many, are forgiven—for she loved much. But he who is forgiven little, loves little" (Luke 7:47).

The prostitute turned Jesus-follower had a deep, intense, overwhelming love for Jesus. Why? Because she was simultaneously aware of her many, many sins and of the deep, deep forgiveness of Jesus. She knew just how evil she truly was. But even more than that, she knew that Jesus had forgiven all of her evil deeds. Her intense experience of forgiveness from Jesus created intense love for Jesus.

If we're going to know God as he truly is, we must know ourselves as we truly are. We must be willing to look unflinchingly at our own wickedness. We need to strip away our nice, Sunday best and peer into the depths of our souls. We won't truly understand how great God's love is until we understand the depths of our wickedness. We won't passionately love God until we understand the magnificence of God's forgiveness.

If you're having trouble grasping your wickedness, simply look to the cross. At the cross we see our sin in all its grotesque, perverted colors. Our sin was so abominable, so offensive, so horrendous, that it required the death of God himself. God's wrath burned so hot against our sins that only God himself could appease that wrath. As Jesus considered the wrath awaiting him, he fell to the ground and began to sweat blood. As he pondered the darkness that would engulf him, he asked God if there was any other way. But there wasn't. The death of 10,000 angels could not atone for our sins. The blood of bulls and goats could not atone for our sins. Only the death of Jesus Christ, the sinless Son of God, the One adored by angels, the second person of the Trinity, could adequately pay for our sins.

As Jesus hung on the cross, our sins were heaped upon him. Our impatience. Our lust. Our envy. Our gossip. Our love for praise. Our addiction to porn. Our adultery. Our neglect of our children. Our divisiveness. Our masturbation. Our homosexuality. Our cursing. Our violence. Our anger. Our sins were so disturbing and grotesque that the Father turned his face away from the Son. Our sins distorted and ruined the Son to such a degree that the Father could not bear to look upon him any longer. The Father was revolted and disgusted by his once-beautiful Son.

The cross is no trifling matter. It is not simply something we wear around our necks and plaster on our Bible covers and give lip service to. The cross shows us our deep sins and God's deeper grace.

There is something very freeing about coming to terms with our depravity. We can stop trying to impress others. We can stop worrying about what other people think about us. We can be okay with criticism. The cross has shown us who we truly are, and it's much worse than we think. But the cross has also shown us who God is, and he's better and bigger and more loving than we could possibly imagine.

Knowing just how evil and bent and twisted we are apart from God also allows us to stop trying to earn our way to God. I could not earn my way to God. Ever. Apart from God, I am too wicked, too evil, too twisted, too perverted, too self-serving, and too weak to do enough righteous works to get to God. I am a spiritual prostitute who will throw myself at every passion that catches my fancy.

But God has done what I couldn't. He came looking for me as I wandered the darkened streets. He came searching for me as I stumbled through the wasteland. He found me, took my head in his hands, and he breathed spiritual life into me. He removed my wandering, whoring heart and replaced it with a heart that loves what is good.

Honestly, I don't like spending time with needy people. I know that I should, but I don't. I don't like spending time with people whose lives are messy. They require too much time, too much emotional energy, too much work. I want to be around people who have it together and who have something to offer me. I want to be around people who give just as much as they take. When people become too needy, I keep them at arm's length.

Thank goodness God is not like me. I never would have

come after me. I never would have pursued me. I was too sinful, too wicked, too hardened, too angry, too totally jacked up. I was more than needy, and I was more than broken; I was ruined. I had nothing to offer God. He wasn't getting himself a good bargain when he saved me.

You cannot neatly package God's grace. It is extravagant, lavish, overwhelming, astonishing, breathtaking, and beautiful. We serve a God who loves the unlovely and pursues those who hate him. We serve a God whose grace flows downhill toward the lowly and despised. We serve a God who dispenses grace so lavishly that it seems cheap. But grace is not cheap. At least not for God. In order to give grace so freely he had to give up his Son. I can't fathom that kind of God, but I certainly can love him.

CHAPTER 5

THE GOD WHO KILLS PEOPLE

Being a cop ain't easy. I mean, sure, Moses handles all the really tough cases, but we get a crap load (pardon my French) of tough jobs too. Case in point: just last night I got a call for a 407, which is the code for a domestic disturbance. So I arrive on the scene and see two guys screaming at each other. I mean, these guys are really fired up, screaming and spitting and on the verge of throwing punches. If I don't step in somebody is going to lose a few teeth, and then I have to fill out a whole bunch of paperwork which I hate doing.

So I put on my tough guy face and saunter up to the brawlers. "What seems to be the problem here boys?" I say, hoping to diffuse the situation.

"This moron here let his ox loose and it gored my ox to death," says one of the guys, stabbing his finger at the other guy.

"Oh you're full of it!" says the other guy, lunging at him. "You know just as much as I do that your ox was the one who got loose. My ox was acting in self-defense." This set both of them off. They fall to the ground in a whirlwind of robes and beards and punches and dirt.

"Boys, boys!" I say, grabbing them both by the collar and yanking them up. They both glare at me like I've got a wicked case of leprosy. "There's a simple way to solve this," I say. "I'm gonna run a quick background check on both of your oxen. That should clear things up." So I run the background check, and wouldn't you know it: angry man number one has a rap sheet longer than Moses' beard. This isn't his first ox goring incident; it's his third.

These are the kind of things I deal with on a daily basis. I also deal with building contractors trying to cut corners by not building parapets on roofs. I deal with greedy hoarders trying to collect too much manna, punk kids trying to sneak into the tabernacle, masters who busted up their slaves, and the occasional crackpot trying to boil a baby goat in its mother's milk. These are all routine events. I fill out the paperwork, submit it to my superiors, and go on my way. Not exactly thrilling material.

But there are some cases you never forget. Like Nadab and Abihu. I still get nightmares about that case. I wake up at night with my heart racing and my body slicked in cold sweat. See, I was the one who found the bodies. Or what was left of them. I saw them come stumbling out of the tabernacle, screaming in agony, arms swinging wildly, flames eating them alive. They were burned so badly it was difficult to identify them. Because I found the bodies, I had to inform their parents. I still remember their mom, Elisheba, falling to her knees and screaming when I told her about her boys. Aaron, their dad, said to me, "Do you have any idea who did this? You'll find the killer, right?"

How was I supposed to answer? I cleared my throat and stared intently at my sandals, trying to compose my answer. "Well, truth is, we already know who killed your boys."

Aaron looked at me expectantly. "Well, who did it?" he demanded.

"God did."

Okay, time out. Let's step out of my anachronistic ancient Israel version of "Cops" and into the present. Were there beat cops in ancient Israel? Probably not. I've obviously watched a few too many episodes of "Law and Order." But God really did kill people. In fact, the Bible is full of stories about God taking the lives of men and women. Yet for some reason we don't like to talk about these stories. When was the last time you heard a sermon about killing people (talk about a great way to shrink your church)? When was the last time you sang the hymn "We Praise Thee For Thy Killings" (FYI: I don't believe such a hymn exists)? I read to my little girls out of several different children's Bibles. We read about David and Goliath, Daniel and the Lion's Den, and Jonah and the Giant Fish. But all the stories of divine killing have been censored out of the children's Bibles. Why? Why do we have such an aversion to these types of stories? Why do we get queasy, uncomfortable, and somewhat apologetic at the idea of God killing someone? I suspect it's because these stories don't jive with the sanitized version of God we have created. We put bumper stickers on our cars that say, "Smile, Jesus Loves You". We don't have any use for stickers that say, "Watch Out, God Might Kill You". We could sing of his love forever, not his wrath.

The truth is, we don't know what to make of a God who kills people. We don't know how to handle a God of fury and wrath and retribution. To talk about God killing people sounds so barbaric and intolerant and politically incorrect. We live in the age of tolerance and peace and respect and "Coexist" bumper stickers. The idea of a killing God makes us feel at least moderately uncomfortable. Can't we all just get along and love each other and hold hands and sing "We Are the World"? Where's the love, man? Do we really have to talk about all this killing stuff?

If we're going to know God as he truly is, then we must come face to face with the God who kills people. We cannot sanitize God or smooth out his jagged edges. We cannot pick the parts of God we like and discard the rest. We must take

God as he is.

After God executed Nadab and Abihu he said:

> Among those who are near me I will be sanctified, and before all the people I will be glorified. (Leviticus 10:3)

This verse implies that God's fury against Nadab and Abihu wasn't an anomaly or mistake. It wasn't as if God had a divine meltdown and lashed out at Nadab and Abihu, like some moody teenager. No, God's actions were precise and calculated. They were intended to reveal something about God to the people of Israel and to us. So what exactly was God trying to prove? In order to answer that question we need to understand what Nadab and Abihu did that was so wrong.

Nadab and Abihu were priests. They were responsible for performing priestly duties on behalf of the people of Israel. They offered sacrifices to God, burned incense before the Lord, and offered worship to the Lord. These were incredibly sacred duties that could not be taken lightly. To enter into the presence of the true and living God was serious business. Not just anyone could come traipsing into the presence of the Holy One. Only those who had been specifically appointed by God could come, and they could only come if they followed the strict instructions given by God.

Why was God so particular about who could come into his presence and how they could come? Because God is holy and human beings are sinful. Holiness and sinfulness cannot mix. God's burning, white-hot righteousness cannot tolerate the tiniest hint of sinfulness. Sin is vulgar, repulsive, and abominable to God.

God created an elaborate system of sacrifices and cleansing rituals for the people of Israel. These sacrifices and rituals would temporarily absolve the Israelite priests of their sins and allow them to minister before the Lord. These rules and rituals were not optional, they were a matter of life and death. When God described the garments that were to be worn by the High Priest, he insisted a bell be attached to the hem of the priest's robe. Why?

> And it [the bell] shall be on Aaron when he ministers, and its sound shall be heard when goes into the Holy Place before the Lord, and when he comes out, so that he does not die. (Exodus 28:35)

To come into the presence of God was no trifling matter. To come into the presence of God was to flirt with death. When God had descended on Mount Sinai, the people of Israel were instructed to stay far away from the mountain. If they even touched the holy mountain, they would be executed. And yet Nadab and Abihu thought they could play fast and loose with God. They thought they could worship God however they wanted. They were under the impression that coming into the presence of the Holy One was no big deal. In Leviticus 10:1 we read:

> Now Nadab and Abihu, the sons of Aaron, each took his censer and put fire in it and laid incense on it and offered unauthorized fire before the LORD, which he had not commanded them.

No big deal, right? Yeah, Nadab and Abihu offered some sort of unauthorized incense before God, but they were just trying to worship God in their own way, right? Did they make a mistake? Probably, but come on. It was just a little bit of incense. Surely God would understand. As we like to say these days, "To each his own." Some people worship God in a church, some people worship God in a trout stream, some people worship God through meditation. God is cool with all this, right?

Nadab and Abihu found out the hard way God was not okay with their worship. "And fire came out from before the LORD and consumed them, and they died before the LORD." (Leviticus 10:2) One minute Nadab and Abihu were swinging their censers of incense, the next minute they were swallowed by holy fire.

Only the High Priest, Aaron, was allowed to offer incense before the Lord in the Holy of Holies, and only with sanctified, sacred censers. Nadab and Abihu knew all this. Their fatal mistake was they didn't take God seriously. They came into the presence of God lightly, without giving thought to who God really was. They forgot that their God was the same God who killed the firstborn Egyptians, obliterated the world in a flood, and drove Adam and Eve out of the garden. God is not a trinket or toy to be played with and tossed about. The worship of the living God is a deadly serious thing. They took God lightly and paid for the mistake with their lives. They laid their unauthorized fire on the altar and were immediately destroyed by God's fire.

Nadab and Abihu weren't the only ones who treated God lightly and paid for it with their lives. Uzzah made the same fatal mistake.

The story of Uzzah is even more baffling to our modern sensibilities than the story of Nadab and Abihu. The setting was one of happiness and hoopla and celebration. The Ark of the Covenant, which represented God's presence with the people of Israel, was finally being returned to Jerusalem after it had been captured by the Philistines. King David, along with the rest of the Israelites, were in a raucous, joyful, celebratory mood. They were all singing and jamming out on harps and smashing cymbals together. It was a Super Bowl parade and a rock concert and a holy Mardi Gras all mashed together.

Uzzah and his brother Ahio were driving the cart that carried the Ark. As the Ark was moving toward Jerusalem, one of the oxen pulling the cart stumbled. I imagine that things went into slow motion at that point. The ox tripped, the cart wobbled, and the Ark began to fall off the cart. In an instinctive and seemingly noble moment, Uzzah reached out and grabbed the Ark of the Covenant to prevent it from falling to the ground. This seems like the right thing to do, doesn't it? The Ark of the Covenant was a sacred thing. Uzzah was doing everything he could to prevent the Ark from hitting the ground. I probably would have done the same thing. But Uzzah made the wrong move.

"And the anger of the LORD was kindled against Uzzah, and God struck him down there because of his error, and he died there beside the ark of God." (2 Samuel 6:7)

What? How could this happen? Uzzah was trying to save the Ark and it cost him his life. By all appearances, he was trying to do a good thing. The Ark was about to fall into the dirt and Uzzah reached out to stop it. And yet the second his hand touched the Ark, God struck him dead. Why? What did Uzzah do that was so bad? Isn't God a God of love and forgiveness and mercy?

Uzzah's great mistake was that he tried to mix the sacred with the sinful. God had made it clear to the Israelites that the Ark of the Covenant was never to be touched. By anyone. Ever. The Ark was to be supported by long poles, which would allow it to be carried from place to place. But the Ark absolutely could not be touched by human hands. Why? Because humans are sinful and God is absolutely holy. The sacred and the sinful can never inhabit the same place. If a person even touched the Ark of the Covenant, they would be defiling the Holy Presence of God. Uzzah touched the Ark and defiled it. God responded in turn by executing Uzzah.

I'll admit, part of me rises up in protest when I read the story of Uzzah. Can't the guy catch a break? A simple reading of his story makes it seem like Uzzah was just a good guy trying to do a good thing who happened to be caught in the wrong place at the wrong time. I almost want to apologize on behalf of God, like I'm embarrassed by God or something. I want to say, "Yes, God killed Uzzah, but God is really loving too. This was sort of a weird fluke accident kind of thing. My God isn't really like that."

Except God *is* like that. His response to Nadab and Abihu and Uzzah was not a fluke response. God doesn't lash out. He doesn't get pushed to the breaking point and then suddenly snap. God doesn't get into bad moods and then take out his anger on other people. God's response was fully calculated and fully just. He gave Nadab and Abihu exactly what they deserved. Uzzah received full justice. The Judge of all the earth did what was right and good and appropriate. If God had allowed Nadab or Abihu or Uzzah to live, the angels would have cried out, "No that's not right!"

The fact that protest rises within me shows I don't fully understand God's holiness or my sinfulness. If a judge pardoned a serial rapist, I would be furious. I would demand the resignation of the judge and the immediate punishment and possible execution of the rapist. I would never fault a judge for sentencing a serial rapist to death. And yet how quickly I rise up in protest against God for his actions. How quick I am to apologize on behalf of God, saying, "No, no, no, God isn't really like that." How quick I am to remind people of God's love over and above his holiness. But maybe I need to stop apologizing for God and start letting God be God. Maybe I need to come face to face with the God of sharp edges and swift justice.

But coming face to face with a holy and just God is a terrifying thing. The prophet Isaiah caught a glimpse of God in the temple. He saw the angels circling God, covering their eyes and crying out, "Holy, holy, holy, is the Lord of Hosts." He felt the temple shake and buckle and saw smoke rising all around him. When Isaiah saw and heard and felt these things, his first instinct was to call down prophetic curses upon himself. He cried out in despair, "Woe is me! For I am lost." Isaiah was a prophet, and as a prophet he normally reserved the word "woe" for proclaiming God's judgment on others. When Jesus said, "Woe," to the Pharisees, he was calling down God's judgment on them for their horrendous hypocrisy. When Isaiah said, "Woe to the wicked," he was calling down God's righteous judgment upon those who rolled and reveled in wickedness.

But when Isaiah came face to face with the living God, he called down God's judgment upon himself! His soul was laid bare. All his defenses were demolished and all his excuses were dashed to pieces. Isaiah proclaimed that he was totally and completely undone. He was suddenly aware that God was very, very holy and he was very, very defiled. He could not offer up any righteous deeds to appease God. The only right thing for Isaiah to do was to call down God's righteous wrath and judgment on himself. Some preachers have a reputation as being hellfire and brimstone preachers, always talking about God's judgment on the wicked. But Isaiah did things in reverse. When he saw God, he called down hellfire and brimstone upon himself.

Isaiah wasn't the only one who was undone in the presence of God. When John the Revelator saw the risen Jesus, he fell down as though he were dead. Annanias and Sapphira weren't even given the chance to fall on their faces. When they lied to the Holy Spirit, they were killed on the spot by God, just like Nadab and Abihu. When Korah wanted to try his hand at doing the priestly work assigned to Moses and Aaron, he and his entire family were literally swallowed by the ground.

All this talk of God killing people raises a rather uncomfortable question: why not me? Why am I still breathing? Why hasn't God taken my life yet? Every day I talk to God like it's nothing! I just stroll into his presence and talk to him. I tell him about my struggles. I ask for his provision. I ask him to take care of me and my children. But I get really distracted too. While I'm praying I also think about football and video games and how tired I am. I don't offer any incense or sacrifices. I don't have a priest pray on my behalf. I go straight into God's presence myself, with all my faults and failures and wickedness. I should be struck dead, or at least be given leprosy like when King Uzziah strolled into God's presence and tried to offer his own incense.

I go to church on Sundays and I worship. Well, I try to worship. But I get distracted by a million little things, like the worship leader missing an intro or a kid dumping Cheerios onto his seat or a lustful thought intruding into my mind.

And I'm usually tired to boot. I would hardly say I'm worshiping God with all my heart, soul, mind, and strength. I may sing "Holy, holy, holy," with my mouth, but my mind is a thousand miles away. Don't get me wrong, I really do want to worship and love and serve God. But what I offer to God is so half-hearted, self-centered, and stained with sin. How can it possibly be acceptable to God? If God killed Nadab and Abihu for offering unauthorized incense, why hasn't he killed me for offering only a tiny bit of my heart?

If Nadab and Abihu were alive they would be baffled. Isaiah would probably be instructing me to call down divine judgment upon myself. And if it weren't for verses like Hebrews 10:19-20, I would most certainly be dead by now. Those verses say:

> Therefore, brothers, since we have confidence to enter the holy places by the blood of Jesus, by the new and living way that he opened for us through the curtain, that is, through his flesh...

Woah, woah, hold on a second. Confidence to enter the holy places? Nadab and Abihu confidently entered the Most Holy Place and were killed because of their audacity. Uzzah touched a holy place and divine judgment fell upon him. Isaiah stood in the holy places and called wrath down upon himself. Korah tried to push his way into the holy places, and God caused the ground to swallow him up. And yet this verse tells us to enter into the burning, white-hot, brilliant, deadly holy places with confidence. This command is absolutely stunning.

How is it possible for us to enter the holy places with confidence and not dread? How is it possible for me to pray to God and worship God and serve God without fear of wrath or retribution? How can I approach the Holy One and not be consumed by fire? It's possible because the divine judgment that should fall on me fell on someone else. The ground that should swallow me swallowed someone else. The death that should consume me consumed someone else.

As Jesus hung on the cross, the horrible wrath and judgment for all our sins fell upon Jesus. God said to Jesus, "Woe to you! Woe to you for your adultery and arrogance and pornography and elitism and hypocrisy and judgmentalism and gossip and slander and gluttony and child molestation and lying and greed and pride and murder and rape and self-centeredness! I will undo you for these sins! I will destroy you for this wickedness. I will unleash my holy, burning wrath upon you!" The divine fury and retribution that belonged to us was heaped in great black mounds upon Jesus. The Judge of all the earth, the Great Executioner, gave justice to Jesus instead of us.

As breath deserted Jesus, the great curtain which separated the Most Holy Place from the rest of temple was ripped from top to bottom. God himself was making a public declaration that the holiest of all places was now open for all who wear the robes of Christ's righteousness.

And then the death that took Nadab and Abihu and Uzzah and Korah also took Jesus. The earth from which we were formed and to which we return swallowed up its Maker. The wages of sin is death, and Jesus received the full wages for our sins.

But death could not keep its raspy talons around Jesus for long. The stone was kicked aside and Jesus strode forth: victor, death-eater, darkness destroyer, conqueror of Hell, conqueror of Heaven. The demons shuddered and the angels rejoiced. The prophets of old who had long peered into this mystery said, "Aha!" Jesus then strode boldly into the presence of God, the holy place, and said, "Father, I am here! I have come to claim my reward. And I bring all those I have clothed in my righteousness."

And the Father said to Jesus and to me and to you, "Welcome Son. Inherit the joy of your Master!"

The corpses of Nadab and Abihu and Uzzah should remind us of just how fearsome our God really is. We do not serve a tame God. We do not serve a God who lets wickedness go unpunished. We do not serve a God who lets himself be pushed around. We do not serve a God who lets anyone come waltzing into his presence. No, we serve a ferocious, holy, righteous, politically incorrect yet fully just God who will not tolerate the tiniest hint of defilement. Those who think they can approach God based upon their own righteousness will end up as a charred corpse. If you have the guts to push your way into God's presence, make sure to attach a bell to the leg of your pants. When it stops ringing your friends can know it's time to collect your body. Those who think they have what it takes to get into God's presence on their own will be subject to punishment by divine execution.

But for those of us who have wrapped ourselves tightly in the righteousness of Christ, the holy places stand open. The thick curtain that once reminded people to stay out of the holy places is now in tatters, and our Father says, "Come in!" We can come and offer our worship, no matter how frail or paltry, without fear of divine judgment, because divine judgment fell on another. Jesus transforms our simple prayers and service from unauthorized fire into sweet incense. God invites us to come into the place where prophets feared to tread. The angels cover their eyes as they circle the throne. God invites us to look upon him with unveiled faces.

Does God kill people? Absolutely. In fact, he killed the One most precious to him so that he wouldn't have to kill us.

CHAPTER 6

THE GOD WHO GIVES HIMSELF AWAY

My generation is infatuated with authenticity. We want to eat authentic, organic, farm to table food which hasn't been defiled by pagan preservatives or that Molech of all food demons, MSG. If you say you like Velveeta Cheese or artificial sweetener, people look at you like you said you enjoy eating puppies or baby deer. We like watching indie movies that aren't polluted by big budgets, massive special effects, and high-maintenance celebrities. Clothing stores pander to our authenticity fetish by making clothes which are already broken in, complete with prefabricated holes. Everyone and their mother uses social media, exposing the most intimate, authentic details of their lives on a minute by minute basis. The really authentic folks listen to bands no one has ever heard, bands who haven't been polluted by money or fame and are still making authentic music. For some reason, a high percentage of these bands seem to come from Sweden and Norway.

Us Christians aren't immune to the authenticity bug either.

Every few days someone writes a blog post in which they rend their virtual garments over the shallowness of the Church. These authors almost always urge everyone to participate in true, authentic community, whatever that means. Hymn zealots get riled up about the shallowness of modern praise songs, and contemporary worship lovers accuse the hymn zealots of being too cold and formal. Everyone wants everyone else to be more authentic and honest and transparent and open about their struggles and faith. Talking about and lamenting your own spiritual "brokenness" is considered to be the true mark of the authentic person. The unforgiveable sin for my generation is hypocrisy. We'll forgive and overlook a lot of sins, but hypocrisy is not one of them.

Personally, I think authenticity is a tad overrated. I mean, sure, transparency and integrity and confession can be good and healthy when done correctly. And I'm all for authentic community, even though no one seems to know exactly what it looks like. I suspect authentic community is to Christians what truth is to philosophers: we're always talking about it, but we never really get it. I realize this kind of talk makes me sound anti-confession and anti-fellowship and anti-all those good things we're supposed to do in church. But I'm really not.

It's just that there are a few things you need to know about me. Generally speaking, I don't like people. I know, I know that sounds awful. It makes me sound like some sort of psychopath or crazy hermit. But it's true. See, most people I know, including myself, have a lot of problems. We've all got marriage problems and health problems and kid problems and car problems and faith problems. I suppose the authentic thing to do would be to confess my problems, roll around in them for awhile, and then listen intently as other people roll around in their problems. But I've never been a big fan of that sort of thing. Honestly, I don't really like dealing with other people's problems. I've got enough problems of my own. In fact, I don't like dealing with needy people in general.

Needy people require time and resources and emotional investment and phone calls in the wee hours of the morning and the occasional bailing out of jail. Being around them is draining. I would rather be around people who have something to offer. You know, funny people or smart people or popular people or rich people. People who make me feel good about myself. People who let me be a burden to them instead of the other way around. I know all this makes me sound like a heartless, selfish person but I'm just being authentic, and that's what it's all about right?

Another reason I'm not a raving fan of authenticity is it forces me to take a hard look at myself, and I don't usually like what I see. I see a lot of selfishness. I see a lot of terrible thoughts about other people. I see a lot of arrogant, snobbish behavior. When I see the sniveling, self-centered, self-exalting, idolatrous thoughts that course through me, I cringe. I regularly battle lustful thoughts, angry thoughts, destructive thoughts, gossipy thoughts (and words), and malicious thoughts. I guess you could say I have a lot of skeletons in the closet of my soul. This whole authenticity business forces me to throw open the closet and air out the skeletons. I'd rather not do that if given the choice.

I guess what all this boils down to is I don't like needy people, yet I am a needy person. I don't like people with a lot of problems, but I am a person with a lot of problems. It's the whole, "I have met the enemy and the enemy is me," business.

What exactly am I driving at? Why have I spent the last few pages spewing my emotional dribble all over the place? Was all this really necessary? What I'm driving at is this: if I were God, I wouldn't like me very much. Like I said, I don't like problematic, needy people, and I certainly fit into that category. If I were God, I would stay as far away from me as possible. I wouldn't have me over for dinner or invite me out to play poker or be my mentor.

But, to my great delight and befuddlement, scripture makes it very clear that God actually really does like me. Not in a generic, God loves everyone because he has to sort of way, but in an intense, personal, parental sort of way. God doesn't just tolerate me like a teacher tolerating a student or a parole officer tolerating a parolee or a relative tolerating other relatives on Thanksgiving. God really, really loves me. Honestly, if God's word weren't so clear about this I would have a hard time believing it were true. That's how grace is. It's too good to be true, but it is true.

In Zephaniah 3:17 God says to his people, "The LORD your God is in your midst, a mighty one who will save; he will rejoice over you with gladness; he will quiet you by his love; he will exult over you with loud singing." Prior to having kids I don't think I could have understood how deep this verse runs. Having kids causes you to undergo a Grinch-like conversion process in which your heart grows two times larger. Having kids causes you to feel a depth of love and emotion you never felt before. I have a little girl named Gwendolyn who is one and a half. I sing a lot over Gwendolyn. I wrap her tight in my arms, and she lays her head on my shoulder, and I sing this silly baby song to her that goes, "I love you, I love you, morning noon and night, I love you, I love you, you make my world bright." Sometimes Gwendolyn sings the song back to me in her little baby voice. Talk about making your heart go to pieces. When Gwendolyn gets hurt I pick her up and quiet her with my tender kisses and soft speech. When I play music, I pick her up and dance around with her and exult over her with loud singing.

My baby girl doesn't have much to offer me. She is constantly getting into things she's not supposed to, like cupboards and purses and toilets. She requires almost constant attention. If I take my eye off her for a second, she'll be playing with a bottle of Windex. You might say she is a needy, high-maintenance person. And yet I love her with all my heart. I give myself away to her. I sing over her and quiet her and treasure her.

In some small way, my relationship with my daughter reflects God's relationship to me. I am God's son. God quiets me with his love. I need to be quieted by God's love on a regular basis. I get worked up over the budget and the future and the rattling noise my car is making. I'm easily flustered and stressed out. I stumble and stutter my way through life, getting myself into one mess after another. In the midst of my worrying and fretting and flitting about God comes to me as a Father and quiets me with his love. I don't know the future, but I do know my God. I can't create my future, but my Father can. These truths about God quiet me. They calm my skittish heart, which jumps at every loud noise and trembles at life's thunderclaps.

God also exults over me with loud singing. To exult over something is to delight and glory in it. It is the overflow of an extremely happy heart. When a soccer player kicks the game winning goal from fifty feet out, he runs across the field, slides onto his knees, and screams at the heavens. He pumps his fists in joy and rips his shirt off. The crowd jumps up and down and chants and screams for joy. They blow noisemakers and yell and hug and high-five. The player and the crowd exult with loud shouts of joy and singing.

When a band plays their most popular song, the audience rises to their feet and sings along at the top of their lungs. They jump up and down and flail their arms and bounce off each other and hit beach balls around. The band front man, caught up in the moment, takes a running leap off the stage into the outstretched arms of the crowd. Everyone is soaked in a joyful sweat and no one cares. The crowd exults over the band with loud singing and the band exults over the crowd.

God's love for me is a loud, raucous, exultant love. God sings a loud, joyful, loving, boisterous, happy song over me. His song of love for me is the overflow of his happiness with me. He doesn't sing hesitantly, looking over his shoulder to make sure no one is watching. He doesn't sing softly so that only I can hear. He isn't a librarian, quietly informing that I will find the "Love" section behind the "Science" section, and to please be considerate of the other patrons. God is a boisterous carnival worker operating a game in which everyone who plays wins. God sings a loud, exultant song over me for all the heavens to hear.

There's a worship song that describes God's love as a "sloppy wet kiss". I don't like this line because I don't like sloppy, wet kisses from anyone. Sloppy, wet kisses gross me out and make me think of large dogs. But I think the author of the song was trying to capture the essence of God's loud, exultant, overflowing love. God's love is loud and exuberant and joyful and overflowing and intense and personal and I'm running out of words to describe it. God doesn't give out his love in little pinches, he splashes it all over us. God's love isn't like a bread line where you barely get enough and your stomach still aches afterward. It's a colossal, unending feast.

I'm sort of uncomfortable talking about God's love like this. It sounds and feels a little too good to be true. It doesn't take much searching for me to find some pretty dark and depraved corners in my heart. My heart is like a hastily cleaned teenager's room. If you squint, things look mostly clean. Just don't look under the bed or in the closet or in my drawers. You'll find all sorts of dirty stuff if you do. To talk about God quieting me with his love and singing over me with loud, exultant singing seems a bit on the extravagant side. Maybe even a little reckless. Everything, including God's love, in moderation, right? Wrong. We serve a God who absolutely gives himself away.

Romans 5:6-8 says:

> For while we were still weak, at the right time Christ died for the ungodly. For one will scarcely die for a righteous person-though perhaps for a good person one would dare even to die-but God shows his love for us in that while we were still sinners, Christ died for us...

How many people would you be willing to die for? My list is pretty short. It includes my wife, my kids, and…that's about it. Would I die for my country? I hope so, but when it comes down to it, I'm not sure. Let's be honest: I probably wouldn't die for you and you wouldn't die for me. No offense, that's just the way it is. Our love for one another simply doesn't run deep enough.

But God died for me. Wait a second. Back up and slow down. Let's see the instant replay. Surely that can't be right. God. Died. For. Me. No, there must be some mistake. Perhaps the transmission was garbled. You don't know who I really am. See, I'm a sinner. A really *thorough* sinner. I don't love God like I should and I don't love people like I should. I don't just fall short of the glory of God - I'm often aiming in the complete opposite direction. If I were a righteous person who had a lot to offer the world, maybe (and that's a big maybe) I would be worth someone else dying. But I'm not even a righteous person. Heck, if I'm straight up honest most of the time I'm not even a decent person. There is no reason why someone should die for me, let alone the Son of God whom all of heaven adores. If anything I should be dying for the Son of God!

But God is not like me. No, not at all. In God's kingdom everything works backwards. Water flows uphill, the sun sets in the East, and grace is given to the worst of sinners. God loves me so much that he sent Jesus to die for me when I was a sinner. A sinner! Not a righteous person who always loves what is good and does what is just. Not a good person who gravitates toward charity and chastity and mercy. Jesus died for me when I was a wretched, God-hating, darkness-loving sinner. Jesus died for when I didn't care about him dying for me. Jesus died for me when I wasn't worth dying over.

We live in a world of broken promises. Husbands and wives promise to be faithful to the death, only to divorce three years later. Dads promise to make it to the next game, only to be pulled into yet another meeting. Friends promise to stay in touch and then never write. Words are cheap and promises are easily broken. The constant promise breaking makes it difficult to trust anyone. It's easy to be cynical in this world of constant promise breaking. But God doesn't play word games. He doesn't make promises he can't keep. He doesn't just say he loves me; he actually proves it.

Jesus hanging on the cross in my place is proof of God's overwhelming, reckless, tidal-wave love for me. The Son of God was stripped naked and pinned to a cross for me. The Son of God was mocked and humiliated and denigrated for me. The Son of God was tortured for me. The Son of God was crushed by his own Father for me. Why would God allow such a travesty to take place? What could motivate God to do this to his own Son? Only a love of staggering proportions could create the cross. The cross should absolutely obliterate any doubts I have about God's love for me. The cross is historical, objective, unchanging proof of God's deep, intense, personal love for me. Every day my sense of God's love will fluctuate. Some days I will feel a sense of God's love; other days I won't. But God's love for me doesn't change. It isn't fickle or fluctuating. It is steady and strong and steadfast, never changing, never ceasing, never ending. When I don't feel a sense of God's love, my first instinct should be to look toward the cross where God displays his love for me in blood red colors.

God's love and grace are so stupefying and counter-intuitive, the natural instinct is to raise questions and objections. This is why Paul said in Romans 6:1, "What shall we say then? Are we to continue in sin that grace may abound?" Paul understood just how great and free and deep God's grace really is. Grace really is completely and truly free. God doesn't stop pouring grace into our lives when we sin. God doesn't weigh out our good deeds and bad deeds each week and then dispense the amount of grace we deserve. Rather, every single day God gives us the amount of grace Jesus deserves. We are wrapped in the righteousness of Christ and every day we receive the blessings due to Christ. Paul understood that preaching truly free grace could lead a person to think they can live in sin. That's how amazing and how free God's grace is. We haven't truly preached grace in all its freeness until people say, "Soooooo, does this mean I can keep living in sin?"

We don't like people who take advantage of free things. When someone takes advantage of the welfare system, we look down on them. We get angry that our tax dollars are being used to support a deadbeat. "Get a job, you loser!" we say. When someone takes advantage of workman's compensation, we think of them as a cheater. Yeah, free is good and all, but don't you dare start abusing the system. The moment you start taking advantage of something free, you are a lazy, hypocritical cheater who doesn't deserve free. You can have free, but you need to earn it. You need to be looking for a job while you're on welfare. You need to be resting up while you're on workman's comp so you can get back to work. In our democratic, work-your-way-to-the-top society, we are very uncomfortable with freeloaders.

I tend to think of God's love and grace like the welfare system. I often feel like I should put up fences around God's love. Sure God loves me, but I need to maintain a certain level of holiness in order to stay within God's love. If I really embrace God's love in all its abundant freeness, I might start thinking I can sin. I might start abusing the system or something. I might start doing wild, crazy, sinful stuff, like those Amish kids who go out into the world to "sow their wild oats".

The reality is, I'm not going to make any progress in holiness until I first embrace God's love for me in all its abundance. God loves me, delights in me, sings over me, and quiets me with his love. Period. No "ifs" attached. No "as long as" clauses in fine print. He is my Father and I am his son. My relationship with him is the product of the finished work of his Son. I cannot *add* to that work; I can only *enjoy* it. I cannot *improve* that work; I can only *rest* in it. God insists on giving himself away without charge. I insult his generosity when I doubt the love of God or try to tack my own good works on to the completely finished work of Jesus.

Isaiah 55:1 says, "Come, everyone who thirsts, come to the waters; and he who has no money, come, buy and eat! Come, buy wine and milk without money and without price." Only those who are thirsty can come drink from God's waters of eternal life. Those who bring a bucket full of their own polluted, defiled waters, intent on adding to God's waters, will be turned away at the door. Only those who are totally broke and have no money can buy God's bread of eternal life. Those who bring their dirty pennies to God insult his generosity and demean the price of God's love. He isn't interested in our rusty buckets and dirty pennies. God's love cannot be bought like some trinket at a flea market. Only God himself could afford his love, which is why he insists on giving it away.

In order to truly love and follow God, I must come to terms with the fact that I am a spiritual beggar. I am flat-out broke and desperately thirsty. I've got nothing to offer God. I must take advantage of him. I don't have a two-way relationship with God, in which we both give and take. No, he does all the giving and I do all the taking. The reason it is more blessed to give than receive is because it is a model of my relationship with God. God does all the giving and I do all the receiving. There is no bartering with God. I don't offer him two weeks of prayer and obedience in exchange for two weeks of blessing. I come to God a dirty beggar with empty hands. I leave a son loaded down with blessing. I come to God thirsty and spiritually dehydrated and leave refreshed and overflowing.

C.S. Lewis talked about how God's grace turns us into "jolly beggars".[vi] I can't think of a better phrase to sum up my relationship with God. I am a beggar. I come to God empty, dry, dirty, brittle, and thirsty, not having anything to offer him. But unlike most beggars, who always seem to have a cover story for their neediness (lost job, sick child, ruined car, etc.), I don't need to have a cover story when I come to God. My neediness is precisely what qualifies me to come to God. I can cheerfully come to him, knowing he will cheerfully give me all the grace I need without slapping me around or telling me to get my act together.

Jesus spent a lot of time hanging around with bad, wicked,

needy people. Mark 2 tells the story of Jesus eating dinner in his house with "many tax collectors and sinners". Tax collectors and sinners were the bad crowd in Jesus' day. Tax collectors worked for the pagan Roman government and cheated honest people out of their money. They were greedy and selfish. Sinners were the type of people who slept around and had affairs and got drunk and lied and got into fights. Moms told their kids not to drink, chew, or run with tax collectors and sinners. The Pharisees and scribes, who were generally considered to be righteous, holy, upright men, stayed as far away from tax collectors and sinners as possible, lest they be defiled. When Pharisees and sinners crossed paths, the Pharisees would reverently look to the heavens and thank God they weren't like those awful sinners.

But Jesus wasn't like the Pharisees and scribes. He waded into the midst of all the tax collectors and sinners. He hung out with them and ate dinner with them and ministered to them and blessed them. Jesus offered himself freely to those who had nothing to give in return. He extended love and grace and mercy to people who had never experienced any of those things. When the scribes saw Jesus eating with the tax collectors and sinners, they were disgusted and offended. They couldn't believe that a supposed holy man like Jesus would even go near such an ungodly crowd. They said to Jesus' disciples, "Why does he eat with tax collectors and sinners?" They were perplexed by Jesus' behavior. Did he have any idea who he was allowing into his house?

It turns out he did. When Jesus heard the disciples talking to the scribes, he interrupted and said, "Those who are well have no need of a physician, but those who are sick. I came not to call the righteous, but sinners." (Mark 2:17) The Pharisees and scribes had it all backwards. They assumed God would only save and bless those who were righteous. Who had it all together. Who regularly attended the synagogue and tithed to the penny and maintained the appropriate beard length. But they had God all wrong. God sent his Son into the world to rescue those who were most needy and desperate. Jesus came to save those who weren't righteous at all. Who didn't have it all together. Who were at the end of themselves. Who knew they were sinners and acknowledged their desperate need for God. Jesus came for the spiritual dropouts and losers and failures and fools. He came to save the lowly and the downtrodden. Jesus absolutely will not save the self-righteous. He will only save those who acknowledge their total emptiness and desperation. I'm glad Jesus came to save sinners because that's what I am: a really sinful sinner who needs a really powerful Savior.

In church, we like to talk about coming to Jesus "just as we are". That phrase sounds so nice and comforting and old-fashioned. We'll gather together for a hymn sing, and we'll come to Jesus just as we are. Then we'll have some cornbread and grits like grandma used to make.

But coming to Jesus just as I am isn't optional. He came to save sinners. I can come to Jesus as a desperate sinner or not at all. There is no middle ground. And yet this is so hard to get into my head and heart. With my lips I acknowledge that I am saved by grace, but I live my life like I'm saved by works. It's like I believe Jesus saves me but my good works somehow keep me on good terms with God. What a joke!

I'm not saying holiness doesn't matter. It most certainly does. But holiness must be built upon the foundation of absolutely free grace. If I try to insert one ounce of my works into that foundation it will crumble. I must stand on Christ the solid rock and nothing, nothing, nothing else. Any foundation other than Christ will crumble under the massive weight of God's righteous requirements. It's Christ or nothing.

I began this chapter by saying I don't like needy people. I'm really glad God isn't like me. He likes needy people. In fact, he loves needy people. In fact, he saves needy people. In fact, he only saves needy people. And I'm a needy person who needs saving.

CHAPTER 7

THE GOD WHO IS NOT IMPRESSED

Artist Andy Warhol famously said everyone gets fifteen minutes of fame in life. Back in the day you were most likely to get your fifteen minutes of fame in one big dollop. You rescued someone from a burning house and made the front page of the paper. You took a bullet on the battlefield and came home to an honest-to-goodness war hero parade, complete with confetti and pretty girls and the key to the city. Or, if you knew how to play the guitar, you could form a band. If your band was decent, you might achieve some local notoriety and even get to open for a big name act.

But the nature of fame has changed in recent years. The slot machine of life still dispenses fame to lucky winners, but now it is dispensed in one second increments. I post something funny on Facebook or Twitter. Lots of people like it and repost it and "LOL" it. For a brief moment I am the center of attention, a blip on the radar of people's consciousness. I feel important and witty and well-liked. For a split second I actually feel like a somebody, like a person who matters, and I feel really good. Then my one second of fame fizzles out, and people turn their attention elsewhere.

But that brief hit of fame was intoxicating, and I want more. So I keep playing the slots, hoping to line up the sevens. I keep yanking the lever of life, hoping to hit the fame jackpot. I post funny status updates and pictures. I post thoughtful "insights". I post commentary on world events. Whatever happens, I can't stop posting. If I stop for even a brief second, people might forget about me. They might forget how important and witty and insightful and spiritual I am. Social media is a great way for me to constantly remind people that I still matter. That I still exist. That I'm still important. I guess you might say I'm a fame junkie, always looking to score my next fix.

And my addiction to fame isn't limited to social media. Generally speaking, I want people to be impressed with me. I want people to marvel at my children. I want people to comment on how well behaved and respectful and wonderful they are. I want people to say, "Gosh, you must be quite a parent. I wish my kids were like yours."

I want people to be amazed at my creative abilities. I hope you've highlighted lots of sentences in this book. I hope you've written notes in the margin like "wow!" and "killer!" and "Pulitzer!". I feel really good when someone gives one of my books a positive review, like I'm a respectable author who has the ear of the world.

I want people to want me. I want to be the guy other people want to be around. The guy who makes people laugh and cry and ponder and love life. I don't like going to parties, but if I do go to a party, I want to be the life of it. I want to be in the center. In the spotlight. As crazed announcer Dick Vitale would put it, I want to be the "BMOC" (Big Man On Campus).

Can you relate to my craving for fame? I suspect you can. Maybe you're clawing and fighting and scrabbling your way up the corporate ladder. Maybe you're carving out a reputation as a theology buff. You're the guy who can answer all the tricky Bible questions about eschatology and covenant theology and supralapsarianism (I think that's a theological term). Maybe you're obsessed with your appearance. You spend hours in front of the mirror ensuring every hair is perfectly placed and your makeup is flawlessly applied. Or maybe you really are a mover and a shaker. You're a big shot lawyer or litigator or politician or pastor or doctor or chief executive officer. You've worked your butt off to get to the top, and you're going to do whatever it takes to stay there. Life is one big game of King of the Hill for you.

The reality is all of us desperately want to be impressive. We crave respect and honor and accolades and atta-boy's. We look up to those who have made it big. Who have reached the top. Who have kicked a lot of butts and taken a lot of names. We adore rock stars and comedians and actors and politicians and pastors and principals.

But what does God think of big shots? What does God think of our "impressive" accomplishments? Is he impressed by our creativity or parenting or social media savvy or political astuteness or big salary or heart warming sermons? Is he impressed by the things which impress us?

I don't think so. In fact, I think God gets a good chuckle out of all our huffing and puffing and chest beating. Psalm 2:1-4 says:

> Why do the nations rage and the peoples plot in vain? The kings of the earth set themselves, and the rulers take counsel together, against the Lord and against his Anointed, saying, "Let us burst their bonds apart and cast away their cords from us." He who sits in the heavens laughs; the Lord holds them in derision.

The kings and rulers and El Presidentes gathered together and plotted against God's chosen king. They smoked Cuban cigars, drank expensive barrel-aged whiskey, gave orders to their security teams, and plotted to destroy King David, God's appointed king. And David wasn't the only one. The kings and rulers have always plotted against God's leaders. They plotted against Moses and Saul and David and Solomon and Hezekiah and, finally, Jesus. These rulers weren't a rag tag gathering of has-beens and wannabes at the Lion's Club. These were the power players, the movers, the shakers, the rich, the strong, the seemingly invincible. These were the guys who made it to the top by crushing the skulls of their opponents. They were ruthless, cut-throat competitors who were determined to break free from God and his rule. This was the great nation of Egypt, the powerful Philistines, the mighty Midianites, and the brutal Romans.

So how does God respond to the threats and taunts and plans of the kings? Does he get nervous? Does he get call for backup? Does he crack his knuckles nervously and say, "Look boys, I'm sure we can figure a way to work this out"?

Not exactly. God looks down on the kings, rulers, plotters, and schemers and he laughs. Not a nervous, shifty laugh, but a hearty belly laugh. Why? Because the pompous, bombastic kings are a joke to him. The kings, with their massive armies and security details and chariot brigades and prize fighters and intelligence reports, do not worry God in the least. They do not pose a threat to him. They cannot do anything to stop him. And God is most certainly not impressed by their tough guy act.

And frankly, why would he be impressed? Isaiah 40:15 says, "Behold, the nations are like a drop from a bucket, and are accounted as the dust on the scales…" All the nations put together are nothing more than a drop of water to God. If all the countries in the world banded together to form a billion man army, they would still be nothing more than a drop. A blip. A spatter. A slight mist. When a drop of water falls onto my hand, I flick it away with a snap of my wrist. Drops don't frighten or impress anyone. A drop of water lands on a rock and is burned away by the noonday sun. Drops have a short life.

Oh you're a high-powered lawyer? You're a corporate executive? You're a literary superstar? You're a social media monster? You're the best boss, best parent, best musician, best teacher, best pastor, or best student ever? Congratulations. You are one tiny atom in the drop that makes up humanity. You are a piece of dust that doesn't even register on the heavenly scales.

I realize it's not popular to talk like this in our politically correct, everyone is special, everyone wins, everyone is a unique snowflake society. I don't say this to denigrate or dismiss your accomplishments. I say it because we need a dose of 200 proof reality. We need to step away from the carnival mirror and see ourselves as we truly are. If we're going to truly love God, we first need to see ourselves from God's perspective. Before we can effectively serve God we need to be properly deflated.

I like to think I'm kind of a big deal. Right. Dream on drop boy. Me and all my fellow dust specks are so impressive! God must be blown away by all the dust bunnies we've managed to cobble together. Huzzah to me and my drop and dust companions.

If anyone could have been impressed with himself, it was King Nebuchadnezzar. I mean, seriously, that dude had it going on. Bill Gates and Bono and Oprah want to be like Nebuchadnezzar when they grow up. Bill Gates built a software empire, Nebuchadnezzar built a real empire. Oprah owns a cable network, Nebuchadnezzar owned a nation. Bono writes catchy songs. If Nebuchadnezzar didn't like Bono's songs, he would feed Bono to the lions and find another songwriter who actually had found what he was looking for. Nebuchadnezzar was the real deal. He was at the center of one of the most powerful nations in history.

There was just one problem: Nebuchadnezzar started to believe what all the papers were saying about him. He became a firm believer in himself, both a member and the president of his own fan club. The more he accomplished, he became the bigger his head became. Each military victory and social advance and technological discovery served as a support for his increasingly obese ego. Everyone was impressed with

Nebuchadnezzar and big, bad Babylon. Everyone except one person: God.

One day, Nebuchadnezzar was taking a stroll atop his palace, admiring all he had accomplished. As he surveyed his accomplishments he said to himself, "Is not this the great Babylon, which I have built by my mighty power as a royal residence for the glory of my majesty?" (Daniel 4:30) As Nebuchadnezzar took in the sights and sounds and smells of Babylon, he couldn't help but give himself a shout out. "Look at what I have accomplished! Look at this city and country I have built! I have done this! I am powerful! Stand in awe of me. Bow down before me. Admire me. Adore me."

To which God replied, "Oh, you wanna play that game? You want to see who is the bigger king? You really want to play 'Anything You Can Do I Can Do Better'? Let me show you who the real king is." Before Nebuchadnezzar even finished his grand pronouncement, a voice came from heaven, saying, "O King Nebuchadnezzar, to you it is spoken: The kingdom has departed from you, and you shall be driven from among men, and your dwelling shall be with the beasts of the field. And you shall be made to eat grass like an ox, and seven periods of time shall pass over you, until you know that the Most High rules the kingdom of men and gives it to whom he will" (Daniel 4:31-32).

With just a word, God took Nebuchadnezzar from the top of the world to the depths of insanity. And this wasn't a mild, Prozac might help, kind of insanity. Nebuchadnezzar went into the wild and lived like a wild animal. He put his mouth to ground and ate grass, like a stupid cow. The divinely-induced insanity caused Nebuchadnezzar to go about naked and to let his hair and fingernails grow obscenely long. The big shot king was reduced to living like a filthy animal. The mighty commander of armies became a raving madman. God gave Nebuchadnezzar fame. When Nebuchadnezzar grew fat on his accomplishments, God stripped Nebuchadnezzar of his sanity.

Finally, after many days of mental darkness and living like

a wild animal, God silenced the voices in Nebuchadnezzar's head. God lifted the mental darkness which had engulfed Nebuchadnezzar. His sanity returned to him and brought with it an accurate understanding of reality. Nebuchadnezzar said of the Lord:

> …for his dominion is an everlasting dominion, and his kingdom endures from generation to generation; all the inhabitants of the earth are accounted as nothing, and he does according to his will among the host of heaven and among the inhabitants of the earth; and none can stay his hand or say to him, "What have you done?" (Daniel 4:34-35)

The moral of the story? God is not impressed by our accomplishments or heroics or creativity or well rounded parenting or killer sermons or witty jokes or catchy songs. Even if we rise to the very top, God is still not impressed. He's not impressed with Bill Gates or Usain Bolt or John Lennon, despite Lennon's claim that The Beatles were bigger than Jesus. He's not impressed by you and he's certainly not impressed by me. And he can take away all our accomplishments simply by speaking a word. One minute you're a high-powered real estate agent, the next minute you're a raving buffoon holding conversations with invisible people.

But why did God hit Nebuchadnezzar so hard? I mean, sure, the guy was a bit cocky, but is that such a big deal? In fact, isn't a little confidence a good thing? You've got to have confidence to get places, right?

Exactly right. Confidence is a necessary ingredient for success. But the million dollar question is: what is the source of our confidence?

Nebuchadnezzar was supremely confident in himself. He was confident in his ability to rule a nation and lead an army and build an empire. He was supremely self-sufficient and self-reliant. He didn't thank God for giving him the ability to rule and didn't acknowledge God as the source of all military might. Nebuchadnezzar was extraordinarily deluded. He was stoned on himself. And so God stripped everything from Nebuchadnezzar. God took away Nebuchadnezzar's kingdom, prestige, and mind. God wanted Nebuchadnezzar to be acutely aware of how unimpressive he really was. There is only one King and he will not share the spotlight. Those who try to steal God's spotlight play a dangerous game. If you try to take God's glory you might start hearing voices in your head.

The people of Babel tried to fight their way into the spotlight and paid a brutal price. In Genesis 11:4 the people of Babel said to one another: "Come, let us build ourselves a city and a tower with its top in the heavens, and let us make a name for ourselves, lest we be dispersed over the face of the whole earth." *Let's build a tower that the whole world can see. Let's rise up and show the world who we are. People are going to remember us. We're going to make history, baby! This is our house.*

And so with much hoopla and backslapping and chest bumping, the people of Babel began work on their tower. They were going to climb to heaven. They were going to make people remember their name. They were going to be history makers. And they did end up making history, just not in the way they imagined.

I imagine God got a good chuckle out of their ridiculous attempt to make a name for themselves. Genesis 11:5 says, "And the LORD came down to see the city and the tower, which the children of man had built." The tower, into which the people had poured themselves, was so small and piddly that God had to "come down" to see it. It was like something a toddler might build out of Legos. Can you imagine a toddler saying, "I'm going to make a name for myself with this Lego tower"?

God wasn't impressed with the Babel tower of Legos, and he wasn't going to share his glory with a bunch of fools trying to climb to heaven. So he confused the people of Babel. He scattered them like ashes in the wind. Their unfinished tower was a testament to their insanity. To their littleness. To their colossal unimpressiveness. To the utter stupidity of trying to steal God's spotlight.

God isn't like us. He isn't impressed by those who manage to fight their way to the top. He isn't impressed by rock stars or geniuses or dictators or rocket scientists. He doesn't give a rip about our intellect or accomplishments or Boy Scout badges. I mean, seriously, we're talking about the God who orchestrates planets and oceans and trillions of living creatures. Do we really think we can rise high enough to impress God? Don't count on it.

But we can go low enough to impress God. Isaiah 66:2 says, "But this is the one to whom I will look: he who is humble and contrite in spirit and trembles at my word." It turns out there is a way to impress God, and it involves going down, not up. If I want to catch God's eye, I must fight my way to the bottom. I must humble myself, lower myself, put my face in the dirt. I must make less of myself, not more. I must embrace my littleness, not out of self-loathing, but rather out of intense reverence for the true and living God who sits on the throne and commands the armies of heaven. The proper position for a frail, dependent, small creature like myself is on my knees in humble adoration. Humility isn't some sort of fake attitude we adopt, like the coach who insists his next opponent is fantastic when they really suck. Humility is simply the proper response to reality. God is infinitely great, worthy, glorious, and deserving of praise. I am not. Therefore, I take my shoes off, put my face to the ground, and cry, "Worthy."

There is something very freeing about humility. I can quit trying to impress everybody. Getting to the top takes an enormous amount of effort. Staying at the top is incredibly draining. And once you get to the top, you realize that the view isn't all that great anyway. Humility allows me to quit trying to be a big shot. I can stop reminding the world how important I am. I'm free to be myself, with all my struggles and quirks and imperfections and oddities. I don't have maintain a veneer of impressiveness, which can be quite exhausting. God isn't impressed with me but he loves me anyway. God knows exactly who I am and he still loves me. That's good enough for me.

Humility also allows me to rejoice when others succeed. This is a tough one for me. I don't want others to succeed; I want to succeed! I want to be the one signing the book deals and making the viral videos and getting the online shout outs and speaking at conferences. When others succeed instead of me I'm ticked off because they're getting the praise I so desperately crave.

But humility is all about reality. God uses each person as he sees fit. God has called some to work in the spotlight and some to work behind the scenes. If God calls me to only make a brief cameo and then to live the rest of my days in quiet service, blessed be the name of the Lord. God is impressed by those who humbly play whatever part they've been assigned.

In 2 Corinthians 10:13 Paul says, "But we will not boast beyond limits, but will boast only with regard to the area of influence God assigned to us, to reach even to you." Paul, the great apostle, author of much of the New Testament, and church planter extraordinaire, knew God had assigned him a particular area and amount of influence. He would not strain and strive and stress to go beyond those limits. He would humbly do the work God called him to do.

One day each of us will stand before God to give an account for our life. God won't say, "Well done impressive servant, for you had a lot of Facebook fans and wrote a bestseller and preached awesome sermons and were a charismatic worship leader." No, God will say, "Well done good and faithful servant. You served humbly, often in secret. You visited the sick. You hung out with the lowly. You gave to the needy. You put away chairs after church. I commend you! Enter into the joy of your master!" And that will be enough.

CHAPTER 8

THE GOD WHO CRUSHES SERPENT SKULLS

The end of the world is big business these days. If you play your cards right, mixing a touch of hysteria with a pinch of insanity and a liberal dose of Biblical prophecy charts showing the intersection of the anti-Christ with the rise of the liberal left, you can make quite a name for yourself. Bible teacher Harold Camping caused quite a stir when he confidently predicted that Christ would return on May 21st, 2011. According to Camping, Christ's return would be followed by five hellish months of fire and brimstone and judgment. Finally, on October 21st, 2011, Christ would return once and for all to destroy the world. Camping, along with several thousand devoted followers, spent massive amounts of money on an apocalyptic, turn or burn publicity campaign. They purchased billboards, full page newspaper ads, and radio spots. A man in my hometown plastered his RV with warning signs and parked it in prominent locations. A number of people spent all they had in preparation for the coming doom.

When the rapture didn't occur on May 21st, Camping insisted a "spiritual rapture" had actually taken place and that the world would still come to an end on October 21st. To the best of my knowledge, the world didn't come to an end on October 21st. Everything still seems to be functioning at least somewhat normally. I guess Camping got that one wrong too.

Mad scientist Christians aren't the only ones imagining the end of the world. Post-apocalyptic novels and movies and television shows are all the rage. Depending on who you read and what you watch, the world will be destroyed as a result of: zombies, a superflu, alien invaders, nuclear fallout, vampire attacks, a tornado of sharks (no joke), or some combination of these. Off the top of my head I can think of at least fifteen post-apocalyptic movies, books, and video games.

If you want to snag your own reality television show you can become a doomsday prepper. Doomsday preppers build bunkers, amass firearms, hoard canned goods, and teach their young children how to place three carefully aimed shots into the forehead of an intruder. The doomsday preppers are prepared for the apocalypse. For the financial meltdown. For the invasion by North Korea. For the superflu epidemic. For the nuclear winter. When the world falls apart, they will take refuge in their bunkers. And yes, these folks do have their own reality television shows, which is a sign of the apocalypse in and of itself.

Why is everyone so obsessed with the end of the world? Why is everyone so fanatical about zombies and raptures and nuclear fallout and robot uprisings? Because it's not particularly difficult to imagine the end of the world. If you watch the news for five minutes you'll be assaulted by stories of genocide, rape, murder, government shutdown, terrorist attacks, and rampant poverty. Evil is pervasive and powerful and widespread. It doesn't take much creative prowess to imagine evil getting out of control. People already hurt and kill and exploit each other. Young girls are sold as sex slaves. Pornography rules the Internet. Nasty Internet rumors spread like an airborne disease. Spouses cheat on each other. Hundreds die when a ferry sinks in Thailand. Hundreds of thousands are swallowed alive by a tsunami in Sri Lanka. Evil is everywhere and it is strong. The darkness is deep and thick and suffocating. A cannibalistic zombie apocalypse is only a few steps further. When we see the atrocities which fill the earth, the natural human instinct is to imagine evil completely overrunning the world. It's hard to imagine good triumphing over the millions of horrendous evils which take place every day.

But God doesn't work according to our imaginations. He doesn't play by our rules. The normal laws of cause and effect don't apply to the One who created cause and effect.

Make no mistake, the apocalypse is nigh. God's word makes that fact crystal clear. In the words of Jim Morrison, "This is the end, my only friend, the end." The doomsday preppers and sidewalk prophets got it right. This is the end of the world as we know it (shout out to R.E.M.). However, contrary to the movies and novels and crazies, evil won't carry the day. Darkness won't win. Satan won't have the final word.

Do you remember the Battle for Helm's Deep in *The Lord of the Rings: The Two Towers*? Aragorn, Legolas, Gimli, and the rest of the troops were being overrun by Saruman's massive army of darkness. Director Peter Jackson, who is somewhat obsessed with slow motion shots, showed each of the main characters being slowly overwhelmed by the incredible mass of evil Saruman had unleashed upon them. The situation was hopeless. There simply was no way Aragorn and his troops could win the battle. But as hope faded, Aragorn clung to a simple promise given to him by the powerful wizard Gandalf: "Look to my coming on the first light of the fifth day, at dawn look to the east." Aragorn staked his life and hope on that promise.

On the dawn of the fifth day, when all hope was lost, Aragorn looked to the east. Gandalf appeared on a ridge, seated on his white stallion, Shadowfax. In dramatic fashion,

Gandalf reared back on his horse, then charged down toward the enemy forces of Saruman, leading the Riders of Rohan behind him. The army of Saruman was routed and victory was snatched from the jaws of defeat.

As evil surges all around us, we too have a promise. A promise of hope, of life, of light in the darkness. Of dragons being slaughtered and Serpents being crushed and demonic hordes being routed. And like Aragorn, we must stake everything we have on that promise.

Genesis 3 tells the heartrending story of humanity's plunge into darkness. Satan convinced Adam and Eve to eat the fruit which God had forbidden. Their act of defiance and disobedience opened the gates of Hell. Wickedness surged forth and filled the earth. Every good thing God created was distorted and defaced and marred by sin. On that awful day, all hope was seemingly lost. No one would have faulted God for unleashing his holy fury and destroying everything he created. No one would have blamed God for slaughtering all of creation and beginning afresh. But he didn't do that. Instead, he made a promise. God said to Satan, "I will put enmity between you and the woman, and between your offspring and her offspring; he shall bruise your head, and you shall bruise his heel." (Genesis 3:15)

God allowed Satan to win the battle in the Garden of Eden. But the war was not over. God prophesied the coming of the Serpent crusher. A deliverer. A healer. A rescuer. A holy warrior. A king. A man who would place his foot upon Satan's skull and slowly crush the life out of Satan. Evil would not have the final word. Satan would not have the final victory. The Serpent crusher would come to undo all the sadness and death and despair wrought by Satan.

The hope and longing for a deliverer runs throughout the Old Testament. In Genesis 6:5 we see the absolutely viral nature of evil: "The Lord saw that the wickedness of man was great in the earth, and that every intention of the thoughts of his heart was only evil continually." All of humanity had become sinfully twisted and distorted and grotesque. Every intention, desire, and thought was evil. And their evil actions and desires weren't intermittent blips, they were constant. So God raised up Noah. He placed Noah and his family in that great wooden Titanic and then proceeded to completely destroy the rest of humanity, leaving only Noah. Noah was a second Adam, a new beginning to the human race. Would he be the Serpent crusher? Would he stand for righteousness and purity and uprightness? Would he succeed where the first Adam failed? Nope. Noah departed the ark, offered sacrifices to the Lord, and then got wasted on home brewed wine. Noah was not the Serpent crusher.

But God wasn't done. Unlike us, God always finishes what he starts. He raised up the people of Israel. By the hand of Moses he delivered them from slavery and promised to lead them into a sweet and pleasant land. If Israel would obey God and keep his covenant, he would be their God and they would be his people. Israel was supposed to show the world what the true God was like. They were supposed to manifest the kingdom of God upon the earth. To live holy lives, to love each other, and to worship the living God. God commanded them to drive out evil from their midst and to live consecrated lives. Would the people of Israel be the Serpent crusher? Would they be the ones who finally eradicated wickedness from the earth? Sadly not. As they wandered the Sinai desert, they grumbled and murmured and fumed against God. "Give us something to eat!" they demanded. When they came to the border of the Promised Land, they shrank back in terror, scared witless by the giants who inhabited the land. They believed what they could see rather than the sure, unshakeable promises of God. And so God cursed them to wander the desert for forty years. Israel was not the Serpent crusher.

Maybe a king would be the Serpent crusher. A mighty man of power, influence, and courage. A man who killed giants with stones and pulled off daring raids behind enemy lines. A man after God's own heart. A man like King David. If anyone could crush Satan and destroy the power of evil, it was David. He was the guy who trusted God as he walked through the Valley of the Shadow of Death. He was the guy who refused to kill wicked King Saul even though he had ample opportunity. He was the guy who could exorcise demons simply by playing his harp. But David, just like those who had come before him, failed miserably. He committed extravagant, salacious adultery and then used a black ops murder plot to cover up his tracks. The man after God's own heart also injected more evil into the world.

Perhaps Solomon, David's son, would learn from his father's mistakes. After all, Solomon had a lot going for him as well. God gave Solomon supernatural, mind-boggling wisdom and insight. He gave Solomon unimaginable wealth, power and influence. He allowed Solomon to expand the borders of Israel and to usher in an unprecedented time of wealth and prosperity for the entire nation. He built a glorious temple in which the people could worship God. When the Queen of Sheba came to visit Solomon, she was speechless. The rumors she had heard didn't even tell half the story. For a time, it seemed Solomon just might be the Serpent crusher. God's people were increasing, God's kingdom was expanding, and God's name was being honored. But eventually the power of Satan proved too much for even the great Solomon. The Serpent deceived Solomon, convincing him to marry foreign women even though God had strictly forbidden it. These foreign women persuaded Solomon to abandon the true God and worship foreign gods. Solomon failed. He was not the Serpent crusher.

Put yourself in God's shoes. What would you do? Everyone has failed you. The best and brightest and most godly have turned against you. Together, Satan and humanity have intentionally, maliciously, zealously ruined the wonderful world you created. At what point do you say enough is enough? When someone lets me down once, I can deal with it. Maybe they had a bad day or had a headache or were in a bad mood or their car broke down. To err is human. But when someone lets me down again and again and again, I start to lose patience. If that same person starts intentionally treating me like trash, then I really lose patience. There comes a certain point when one has to say, "I'm not going to deal with this anymore." A person can only handle so much pain and rejection and sorrow and anger and frustration. If I was God I would have washed my hands of this wicked world and all of us wicked people a long time ago.

But God isn't like us. He is faithful to us even when we're not faithful to him. Psalm 103:8 says, "The Lord is merciful and gracious, slow to anger and abounding in steadfast love." To say God is slow to anger is an incredible understatement. Yes, he punished Adam and Noah and Israel and David and Solomon. Yes, he brought judgment on the wicked. But God promised to send the Serpent crusher, and he followed through on that promise in the most surprising way.

The greatest kings failed to crush the Serpent. The greatest spiritual leaders failed to crush the Serpent. The mightiest warriors failed to crush the Serpent. And so God sent a baby.

The Son of God, the One adored by angels and feared by demons, the One who created the universe, the One who sustains every atom and supernova, entered the womb of a peasant girl. The One who upholds all drew life into his tiny body through an umbilical cord. The One who sits in unapproachable light was born into a dark, dank stable. The One who causes hearts to beat took a heartbeat for himself. Psalm 103:14 says of the Lord, "For he knows our frame; he remembers that we are dust." The Son of God took on a human frame. The Son of God became dust.

As Jesus grew, he succeeded where everyone else had failed. While Jesus was in the wilderness, Satan tempted him to make use of his divine power and create food for himself. Satan tempted Jesus to eat. Adam and Eve ate. Jesus did not. Jesus tended to hang with drunkards. Noah got drunk. Jesus remained sober. When Jesus was in the wilderness, Satan invited Jesus to prove his divinity by putting God to the test. Israel didn't trust God and consistently put him to the test. Jesus refused to test God. Jesus also spent much time around women. King David exploited women. Jesus honored women. Satan offered Jesus all the kingdoms of the world. Solomon married foreign women in order to solidify his position of power in the world. Jesus refused every offer of power he received.

Jesus could have had whatever he wanted. He was wiser than Solomon and more powerful than David. He healed the sick, cast out legions of demons, and made the learned Pharisees look like high-school dropouts. Jesus could have been King. He could have delivered Israel from Roman rule, sat upon a throne, and received the adoration of thousands. But in order to crush the Serpent Jesus had to go down, not up. Thousands before him tried to crush the Serpent by rising to the top of the power pile, and all of them had failed. Jesus crushed the Serpent by making himself nothing.

Philippians 2:5-8 says:

> Have this mind among yourselves, which is yours in Christ Jesus, who, though he was in the form of God, did not count equality with God a thing to be grasped, but emptied himself, by taking the form of a servant, being born in the likeness of men. And being found in human form, he humbled himself by becoming obedient to the point of death, even death on a cross.

These verses are astonishing. The Son of God emptied himself. Became a servant. A servant! A servant makes it his ambition to meet the needs of others. A servant puts the desires and interests of others ahead of his own. A servant has no rights of his own. A servant is a nobody. The Son of God became a nobody.

What did Satan think of Jesus becoming a servant? Was he perplexed? Mystified? Befuddled? Satan had no concept of being a servant. He was expelled from heaven for trying supplant God. For clutching and grasping for power. Did he smirk at Jesus? Did he think Jesus a fool for making himself nothing? Did he realize that a deeper magic was at work?

Jesus did not remain a servant. He had to go even lower. He allowed himself to be arrested, mocked, beaten, stripped, humiliated, and rejected. Jagged thorns were mashed down on his head and spikes were punched through his hands and feet. He was hung on a cross, suspended between heaven and earth for all to see. People jeered. The demons rejoiced. The angels wept. A spear was plunged into his side, releasing the blood and water which surrounded his heart. The Son of God was dead. The Life Giver willingly gave up his life. The Creator allowed himself to be executed by those he created.

For a brief moment it appeared that Satan had won. That evil was victorious. That death would be the ultimate victor. That the light was gone. That it would be always winter and never Christmas. That all the hopes and dreams and longings of God's people would never come to fruition. Satan had most certainly bruised the heel of Jesus.

But God never forgets a promise. Satan bruised the heel of the foot that would crush his skull. Jesus told his disciples to look for him on the third day. To watch for the sign of Jonah. To interpret the signs and predictions and prophecies. To look for the Serpent crusher.

On the third day, the dead, spiked hands twitched, the punctured heart began pumping once again, and the bruised heel kicked down the tombstone. The Author of Life allowed himself to be swallowed by death and then fought his way out from the inside. Jesus strode forth from the tomb the victorious conqueror, the holy warrior, the divine rescuer. He had passed every test, beaten every foe. He succeeded where Adam, Noah, Moses, Israel, David, and Solomon had all failed. When the tombstone was flung aside, Satan knew his doom was sure. His greatest weapon, death, had been ripped away from him by Jesus. The wages of sin are eternal death. Jesus paid those wages for all who believe in him. Satan can't condemn those who have tied themselves to the Serpent crusher. Death couldn't hold Jesus and it can't hold those who are bound up in Jesus. When Jesus emerged from the tomb, he placed his foot upon Satan's skull and began to slowly press down.

Jesus isn't done yet. When he rose from the dead, he dealt the death blow to Satan, but he hasn't completely finished him off yet. But that day is coming soon. John the Revelator caught a glimpse of what is to come. "... and the devil who had deceived them was thrown into the lake of fire and sulfur where the beast and the false prophet were, and they will be tormented day and night forever and ever." (Revelation 20:10) Jesus will return in power and glory, and on that day he will bring Satan's reign of terror to a fiery end. He will take hold of Satan, that great deceiver, and he will fling him into the lake of fire. When that happens, we will all lift our voices in a triumphant cheer, and we will bow down before our conquering king. We will salute Jesus, the great Serpent crusher.

Evil will not win. Satan will not have the final say. Though the gloom is great, the darkness will not win. Now we walk through the Valley of Death. Now we mourn and weep and grieve. Now we wage war against cancer and Alzheimer's and Hodgkin's and Parkinson's. Now we lose children in car crashes. And though these trials are brutal, they are not final. They are the dying gasps of a Serpent who is being slowly crushed. They are final thrashes of a dying animal.

God isn't like us. If he was he would have destroyed all of humanity long ago. But he didn't. Instead, he promised a Savior. A Redeemer. A Rescuer. Jesus is that savior, rescuer, and redeemer. He will wipe away every tear from our eyes. He will make all things new. And we will see our Untamable God face to face.

ABOUT THE AUTHOR

Stephen Altrogge is married to Jen. He has three little girls. He drinks way too much coffee and knows way too much about Star Wars. You can find him on the web (www.TheBlazingCenter.com), Twitter (@stephenaltrogge), and Facebook (stephenaltrogge).

[i] Tozer, A.W. (2012). *The Knowledge of the Holy* [Loc 18, 24 Kindle Version]. Retrieved from Amazon.com

[ii] Packer, J. I. (1973). *Knowing God.* Downers Grove, Ill.: InterVarsity Press. Pg 30.

[iii] Martin, D. (2011, May 12). Lady Gaga: 'My tour is a religious experience'.*theguardian.com.* Retrieved December 10, 2013, from http://www.guardian.co.uk/music/2011/may/13/lady-gaga-exclusive-guardian-interview

[iv] Wells, D. F. (2008). *The Courage To Be Protestant: Truth-lovers, Marketers, and Emergents In the Postmodern World.* Grand Rapids, Mich.: William B. Eerdmans Pub. Pg 112.

[v] Bosman, J. (2012, July 5). To Use and To Use Not. Retrieved December 10, 2013, from http://www.nytimes.com/2012/07/05/books/a-farewell-to-arms-with-hemingways-alternate-endings.html?_r=0

[vi] Lewis, C. S. (1960). *The Four Loves.* New York: Harcourt, Brace. Pg 131.

Made in the USA
Lexington, KY
30 September 2016